reading, I feel better prepared for the road ahead and empowered with new insight and coping tools. Beautifully written, easy to navigate with its detailed Contents pages, and easily digestible. A much-needed companion and resource for healing after such profound loss."

— **Dillon S., Dublin, Ireland**

"Another book from Elaine Mallon that hits it out of the park! Easy to read and well organized, *HEALING AFTER THE LOSS OF YOUR PARENTS* is like talking to an old friend. It validated many of my feelings about being an adult orphan. Everyone's experience is different, but Elaine takes that into account when she writes. Thank you for once again helping me feel less alone during a time when I feel so lost."

— **Debbie C., Duluth, Minnesota**

"This book is a tenderhearted and deeply insightful resource for those struggling with the profound loss of both parents. Through its heartfelt narratives and valuable advice, this book offers solace to the grieving, guides them to navigate the overwhelming emotions of heartbreak, identity, and closure. The book's wisdom lies in its capacity to recognize the depth of sorrow while gently enlightening readers toward acceptance, healing, and finding strength in the memory of their loved ones. It is a reflective guide for anyone facing the void left by such a profound loss."

— **Gina A., Rockford, Illinois**

"Elaine Mallon has done it again. She tenderly paints a picture of what grief and the loss of two parents looks like. In my experience, grief is not linear, and as Elaine put it, we will likely go through several setbacks. This book let me know that I am not crazy, and I can grieve in my own way. It is nice to know there is guidance and hope through such painful loss, and I am not alone."

— **Hope T., Glen Burnie, Maryland**

"I love how accurately this book explains the grieving process and this complicated new life stage as an adult orphan. Whether you're trying to cope with the loss of both parents or you are trying to support someone who has, this comprehensive book helps to understand the often confusing psychological, social, familial, and physical impacts of grief. It is definitely a must-read no matter where you are in your grief journey!"

— **Kimberly C., Angier, North Carolina**

"A must-read for anyone navigating the loss of their second parent, re-grieving the first, and all that comes with being an adult orphan. Elaine Mallon has very eloquently put into words all that I am and have been experiencing and has provided a meaningful guidebook that helps traverse this difficult journey. And for those who are walking alongside the grieving, this book is an excellent resource for how to provide invaluable support. It's really good!"

— **Carol-Anne M. R., Edmonton, Canada**

"At a time when most of us feel lost and nothing makes sense, this book provides answers that are easy to understand and apply. This is an excellent companion and guide for anyone trying to rebuild their life after losing their parents."

— **Aiden D., Cedar Rapids, Iowa**

Praise for
HEALING AFTER THE LOSS OF YOUR PARENTS

"This book is a beautifully written and comprehensive guide and companion for anyone trying to find their footing after the loss of both parents. Elaine Mallon has an amazing gift of pulling together lived experience, grief theory, psychology, and spirituality in a really accessible and loving way. The expanse of the book, from the first acute pain of grief to the possibility of finding new life through time and healing, makes this book one to stay on your nightstand for months or years to come. I look forward to revisiting it often and will definitely be using and recommending this book in my grief counseling work!"

— **Nancy Loyd, Grief Support Manager, Grace Hospice, Minneapolis, Minnesota**

"A deep look at what is rarely analyzed or noted in the grief literature—the loss of both parents and the process of self-reinvention that takes place between both deaths. Very helpful in adding to one's knowledge and understanding of the grieving process."

— **Gina S., New York City, New York**

"This book has helped me contextualise this immense feeling of losing both parents. It covers the new life stage amidst losses, re-grieving past deaths, brain trauma, relationship changes, specialist advice, and also advice from those who have already journeyed this path. It's reassuring to know there's an explanation for the crazy emotions you're experiencing. This book is overall a much-needed light in the dark for all of us adult orphans."

— **Sophie G., Brighton, United Kingdom**

"This remarkable book is incredibly inspiring. I gained so much wisdom and insight. There is something magical about the way Elaine Mallon 'speaks' to the reader that brings comfort and sparks self-reflection. I have no doubt many readers will resonate with this important grief recovery guidebook."

— **Liz S., St. Paul, Minnesota**

"Elaine Mallon tackles the loss of both parents with great insight and empathy. Her book is beautifully written, overflowing with great advice and thought-provoking information, and more importantly, the knowledge that we aren't alone. Elaine makes us feel heard and understood. She offers comfort, wisdom, and hope—some things desperately needed after such intense losses. I loved this book and highly recommend reading it."

— **Dori R., Austin, Texas**

"Wonderfully written and resonated with me from start to finish. I couldn't put this book down. This is a must-have resource for navigating this life-altering new stage in life, understanding the grief process, and finding your way forward."

— **Michael G., Sydney, Australia**

"Wow! What an amazing read. I felt like I was reading a road map through grief. This book is a must-read for anyone who has lost both of their parents."

— **Anne H., Pfafftown, North Carolina**

"This is such a comforting and informative guidebook in the wake of double parental loss, like someone holding your hand, making space for your grief when you need it most. After

"This book is a wonderful companion for your journey through grief to healing from the loss of both parents, an experience we will all face. As a medical professional who provided caregiving for both parents, I anticipated grief would come. But despite my knowledge, preparation, and support, it still felt like losing an extremity. This book explains what I am feeling and—using layman's terms—the neuroscience behind our emotions and 'why' we feel so different. It offers coping mechanisms and encouraging ways to heal from losing the longest relationships of my life. Thank you for this gift, Elaine Mallon. This book will impact so many people who seek comfort."

— **Polly A. Porter, Physician Assistant-Certified,
Hillsboro, Virginia**

HEALING
AFTER THE LOSS OF YOUR
PARENTS

HEALING
AFTER THE LOSS OF YOUR
PARENTS

Finding Comfort & Purpose Through This New Life Stage as an Adult Orphan

ELAINE MALLON

GOLDEN LIGHTHOUSE
PUBLISHING

Copyright © 2024 Elaine Mallon
Publisher: Golden Lighthouse Publishing®

First Edition: October 15, 2024

All rights reserved. No part of this book may be reproduced, stored in a retrieval system, or transmitted in any form or by any means—including, but not limited to, electronic, photocopying, or recording—without the prior written permission of the publisher and author, except in the case of a brief quotation embodied in critical reviews and certain other noncommercial uses permitted by copyright laws.

Library of Congress Cataloging-in-Publication Data is on file in the Library of Congress, Washington, D.C.

Hardcover ISBN: 978-1-7335389-7-8
Paperback ISBN: 978-1-7335389-5-4
e-book ISBN: 978-1-7335389-4-7
Audiobook ISBN: 978-1-7335389-6-1

Story Editor: James Endrst
Proofreader: Liz Saucedo
Headshot Photography: Bradford Rogue Photography
Interior Photos: Elaine Mallon

Some names, discussions, and identifying details have been changed to protect the privacy of individuals interviewed. In some cases, composites of individuals have been created.

This book is drawn from the author's personal experience through double parental loss, research on the topic, and interviews with hundreds of people at various stages of the grieving process. Mallon is the author of the Amazon Best Sellers grief recovery guidebook *Healing After the Loss of Your Mother: A Grief & Comfort Manual* as well as the founder of the worldwide online grief recovery support group of the same name.

The content in this book has been carefully researched and all efforts have been made to ensure accuracy. The publisher and author assume no responsibility for any injury or damage incurred as a result of following this information. This book should not be used as a substitute for professional medical or psychological advice. Always consult your doctor or mental health practitioner for your individual needs.

Printed in the United States of America.

Contact and Media Queries: GoldenLighthousePublishing@outlook.com
HealingAfterTheLossOfYourParents.com

"So it's true, when all is said and done, grief is the price we pay for love."

— E. A. Bucchianeri

Dedication

To my fellow wayfarers: No one need walk alone.

To my mother, Irma, and father, Dennis: Love never dies.
I am grateful to you and eternally proud to be your daughter.

Contents

Introduction ·xxiii

Part I: THE ADULT ORPHAN ·1

Chapter 1 Losing Both Parents ·3
           Orphaned · 4
           Difference Between Death of First and
           Second Parent · 7
           Reawakened Grief · 9
           Personal Transformation · · · · · · · · · · · · · · · · · 10
           Identity · 12
           Mortality · 14
           New Stage in Life · 16

Chapter 2 The Grieving Process ·18
           Clarifying the Stages of Grief · · · · · · · · · · · · · · 20
           No "Right" Way · 21
           Four Tasks of Mourning · · · · · · · · · · · · · · · · · · 22
           Growing Around Grief · · · · · · · · · · · · · · · · · · · 24
           Bereavement Your Way · · · · · · · · · · · · · · · · · · 25

Chapter 3 Empowered Grieving ························· **27**
    Grief Work Versus Allowing ················ 27
    Go With the Flow ························ 28
    The Power of Surrender ··················· 28

Chapter 4 Where to Start? ···························· **30**
    Build a Support System ···················· 30
    Relationship Changes ····················· 31
    Guidance Shortlist ······················· 33
    Wellness Routine ························ 34
    Permission to Fall Apart ··················· 35

Chapter 5 Grief Is Messy ····························· **36**
    What Can I Expect? ······················ 37
    Physical ······························ 40
    Cognitive ····························· 41
    Social ································ 42
    Spiritual ······························ 43

Chapter 6 How Grief Rewires the Brain ················ **46**
    Emotional Trauma Is Brain Trauma ·········· 46
    Neuroplasticity ·························· 48
    Grief Brain ···························· 49
    Brain Healing ·························· 51
    "Happy Hormone" Hack ·················· 53

Chapter 7 Grief Versus Depression ···················· **56**
    Prolonged Grief Disorder ·················· 60
    Traumatic Grief ························· 60
    Anticipatory Grief ······················· 61
    Delayed Grief ·························· 62

	Suicidal Thoughts · 63
	When to Seek Help · 65
	Depression as Your Ally · · · · · · · · · · · · · · · · · 66
Chapter 8	**How Long Will This Pain Last?** · · · · · · · · · · · · ·67
	The First Three Months · · · · · · · · · · · · · · · · · 68
	Three to Six Months · 70
	Six Months to a Year · 70
	The First Year & Beyond · · · · · · · · · · · · · · · · · 71
	Long-Term Adjustments · · · · · · · · · · · · · · · · · 72
	Your New Normal · 73
Chapter 9	**Grief Triggers & Glimmers** · · · · · · · · · · · · · · · ·74
Chapter 10	**Holidays & Special Occasions** · · · · · · · · · · · · ·79
	Plan Ahead · 80
	Relieving Pressure · 80
	Family Traditions · 81
	New Customs · 82
	The Holiday Season · 83
	Mother's & Father's Day · · · · · · · · · · · · · · · · · 84
	Your Birthday · 85
	Their Birthdays · 87
	The Anniversaries of Their Deaths · · · · · · · · · · 88
Chapter 11	**Keeping Your Relationship Alive** · · · · · · · · · · · **89**
	Talk to Them · 90
	Bring Them with You · · · · · · · · · · · · · · · · · · · 91
	Storytelling · 92
	Present Tense · 93
	Journaling · 93

	Memory Boxes · 94
	Be of Service · 95
	Memorial Tattoos · 95
	Stepping Into the Parental Void · · · · · · · · · · · · 96

Chapter 12 The Afterlife · **99**
    Crossing Over · 101
    Near-Death Experiences · · · · · · · · · · · · · · · · · 103
    Visitation Dreams · 107
    Signs · 109
    Synchronicity · 114

Chapter 13 Coping Tools, Tips & Strategies · · · · · · · · · · · · **118**
    Mind · 119
    Body · 132
    Soul · 141

PART II: BEREAVEMENT SUPPORT COMMUNITY FORUM · 149

Chapter 1 Walking Each Other Home · · · · · · · · · · · · · · · · · **151**
    The Wounded Healer · 152
    The Comfort of Community · · · · · · · · · · · · · · 153
    Bereavement & Grief Support Group Types · · · 154
    Finding the Right Group · · · · · · · · · · · · · · · · · 156
    Unexpected Benefit · 157

Chapter 2 Peer Community Q&As · **159**
    Losing Both Parents · 160
    Tips & Advice · 163
    Regaining Balance · 168
    Juggling Grief with Closing an Estate · · · · · · · · 172

Caregiver Burnout · 175
Returning to Work · 178
Have You Changed? · 181

Chapter 3 **Healing Roundtable: Advice, Guidance &
Hope** ·184
How Was Losing Both Parents Different
from When You Lost Your First Parent? · · · · · · · 186
How Did Losing Both Parents Affect You?
What Feelings Initially Came Up? · · · · · · · · · · 191
Did it Change Your Inside World
(Identity, Fear of Death, Etc.)? · · · · · · · · · · · · · · 195
Did it Change Your Outside World
(Family Unit, Friendships, Career, etc.)?· · · · · · 199
What Steps Helped You the Most in Moving
Forward Through Your Grief? · · · · · · · · · · · · · 201
Do You Celebrate Holidays and Special
Occasions Differently Now? Did the Loss of
Your Parents Change Your Family Dynamics? · · · 205
What Words or Advice Were Most Comfort
to You in the Early Days After Your Loss? · · · · · 209
What Words, Deeds or Advice Did *Not* Help You? · · ·212
How Long Did It Take to Regain Some
Sense of "Normalcy" Again? · · · · · · · · · · · · · · · 214
Any Words of Advice for Someone Newly
Going Through Double Parental Loss? · · · · · · · · 218

PART III: HOW TO SUPPORT SOMEONE WHO
IS GRIEVING · 223

Chapter 1 **Comfort 101** · 225
Show Up · 226

	Be a Grief Ally	227
	Bear Witness	228
	Holding Space	228
	Grief Is Not a Competition	229
	Getting Started	230
	Empathy	231
	Compassion	231
	Sympathy	232
Chapter 2	What to Do	233
	Practical Assistance	234
	Physical Comfort	236
	Emotional Support	237
Chapter 3	What Not to Do	240
Chapter 4	What to Say	242
Chapter 5	What Not to Say	243
Chapter 6	You Can't Pour from an Empty Cup	246
Chapter 7	The Blessing of a Companion in Grief	248

PART IV: PURPOSE & THE PATH FORWARD · · · · · · · · 251

Chapter 1	The Arc of Life	253
	Life in Stages	253
	I Don't Feel Like Me	254
	The Fear of Dying	256
	Loneliness	259

	The Thick of It	261
	Forgiveness & Moving Forward	262
	Signs You Are Healing	265
Chapter 2	**The Hero's Journey**	**267**
	Make Change Your Friend	268
	Purpose	271
	Meaning-Making	274
	If Not Now, When?	276
	Intention	278
	Positive Motion	279
	Find Your Sunshine	283
	The Wounded Butterfly	284
	Does Time Heal All Wounds?	286
Chapter 3	**Rebirth**	**288**
	The New You	289
	Fly	290
	Acknowledgment	**293**
	About the Author	**295**
	Links & Helpful Resources	**299**
BONUS SECTION		**313**
	Notes to Myself	314
	Favorite Glimmers & Signs	320
	Parental Life Lessons & Advice	326
	Gratitude Journal	332

Introduction

THE FRENCH DON'T SAY, "I miss you." They say, "Tu me manques," which means *you are missing from me*. You are a part of me—a part of my being—that is now gone.[1]

I felt that phrase in my bones the night of my dad's death. He was my second parent to die, which unexpectedly propelled me into a new stage of life—one living with double parental loss.

I felt like an orphan despite being a self-sufficient adult.

Most of us realistically know this day will come, but when it does, it feels surreal—beyond anything our mind seems able to process.

In 2016, my mom—79 years young, healthy, fit, and vibrantly optimistic—suddenly and unexpectedly suffered a severe, ruptured brain aneurysm. I barely had time to catch a 9 p.m. flight from Los Angeles to be by her side at the hospital in Northern California, where she died seven hours later.

My sister, Cari, arrived before me. With little information and still in shock, I walked into the ICU thinking our mother would bounce back in a few days. *She was our all-powerful, superhuman mom, after all.*

"Is she awake?" I asked. My sister shook her head.

But the gravity, for me, wasn't sinking in. I was still in shock and denial.

I spent the next hours talking to my mom, holding her hand, telling her I love her, crying, and playing her favorite songs. As the sun came up, we could see that despite being on life support, her body was shutting down on its own. The severity of the situation became more evident.

There was no hope of recovery.

My mind went back to the last time I embraced her, just weeks before, when I dropped her off at LAX the day after Christmas. I realized that was our last hug. Had I known, I would have held on longer. Tighter.

It was all so confusing and difficult to comprehend. Because she had been in such good health, and both her mother and grandmother had lived to almost 100, I thought she still had decades to live.

I recalled a conversation we had while she was staying with me over Christmas. "You know, if I die," she said casually, "I want you to know it's okay. I've had a great life and wonderful travels. I'll be all right in the next adventure."

She was an idealist, but the candor with which she spoke caught me off guard. Being deeply loving and spiritual, I know in her heart she felt this life is *not* the end. There was no fear in her voice. Still, I couldn't imagine a world without her in it or why she was saying this. I brushed it off, thinking it was not something we'd have to confront for a while.

Then my mind went to our last phone call, which, happily, ended with "I love you." It always did.

Sitting beside her that last morning, those were my last three words to her. It felt like our mother hung on long enough for our goodbyes; to let us know *she* was okay and, being the ultimate mom she was, made sure we had time to prepare ourselves.

She eventually did slip away. It was all so unfathomable. In that moment, it felt like my heart broke in two.

When you love someone with all your heart and you lose them, it really does feel like a literal heart *break*. Half stays with us and half goes with them.

But despite this soul-crushing anguish, it still feels like a solemn honor and privilege to be present when someone makes their transition. In that full-circle moment, I realized my mother was there for my first breath, and, with my sister beside me, I was there for her last.

My mother's death was the worst gut-wrenching pain my heart and body had ever experienced. It was a searing, primal ache so overwhelming it left me wondering how I'd ever survive this life without her in it.

That is understandable. It is said that your first love in life is your mother. Her death, for me in those early days, felt like a part of me died with her.

Experts say the stronger the attachment to the person who died, the more difficult the grieving journey can be. I found that to be true.

Despite the raw, acute pain I felt in those early days, her death didn't kill me.

I did survive.

As we grieve, we slowly learn ways to honor the pain, adapt, rebuild ourselves, and continue forward. But grief, I've learned, never really leaves us entirely. It just changes form.

We never "get over it" because that would mean getting over the love for the ones we lose to death. That is something that will never happen. I'll carry my mom's love in my heart forever.

In the years following my mother's death, I struggled like many people who lost their first parent. On one hand, I was mourning her immeasurable loss while at the same time trying to make sense of my own life and caring for my last surviving, aging parent.

Many who lose their first parent often find themselves in this situation: It can be difficult managing our own grief while balancing the needs of the remaining parent. This was the case for me.

Even though my parents divorced six years prior to my mother's death—after a 52-year marriage—they remained close, and my father grieved as deeply as if they were still together.

It was a hard time for everyone. In the years after, my father struggled with multiple health issues and required more and more attention. My two sisters and I shared the responsibility of caring for him, including grocery shopping, running errands, and giving him the attention and companionship he needed.

In the beginning, I was my father's primary point of care and assigned power of attorney. There were endless trips to doctor appointments, emergency rooms, and hospital visits—in addition to managing his affairs and paying his bills. When he could no longer live alone, and the four-hour roundtrip drive to care for him became untenable, he moved in with my sister for the next two years. I don't know how she managed the level of care he needed at that time, but she did.

Ultimately, we had to place him in a board and care facility when his vascular dementia and Alzheimer's became too severe.

His goodbye was slow. In some ways, I had almost seven years to grieve and prepare because I was losing him slowly, day by day, following his diagnosis. Still, when I got the call that he had died (just three days before the eighth anniversary of my mother's passing), it felt like the world had fallen out from under me.

My response surprised me. I thought being so prepared would cushion me from the pain, but it didn't. I felt the shock, denial, and numbness all over again.

And heartache, just sheer heartache.

We had gone from being told earlier in the day that he was experiencing flu-like stomach pains to the hospice nurse reporting in the early evening that he was now stable. My sisters and I assumed it was another false alarm.

Less than 30 minutes later, my sister phoned to tell me he was dead.

While the course of his decline was expected, his sudden exit was not. We were in a state of disbelief, wondering, "How?" and "Why?" Later, we learned a ruptured stomach aneurysm ended his years of gradual decline.

I didn't get the intimate moment of being by his side when he died, but I know that's the way my stoic father would have wanted it. He was Irish and more emotionally reserved than my mother. It was fitting that he chose the perfect "Irish Goodbye" to slip out without saying farewell.

I did make the two-hour drive to be with his body that night before the funeral home transported him away. When I arrived, it was clear "he" was gone—only the mortal shell remained. His soul no longer animated his body. I sat beside him and combed his hair one last time—just like I did as a kid while we watched TV in the den.

My sister and I played some of his favorite crooner music. I cried and told him I loved him. In that moment, looking at his now thin, frail body in bed, I realized despite any father/daughter issues we may have had in life, he did the best he could.

I felt that deeply in my heart.

When I got home in the early hours of the following day, I sat numbly in my living room. It was difficult to wrap my head around the idea of losing my father.

And then came the cold, hard realization: I had lost both my parents. I felt almost lifeless under the weight of this new reality. In that raw moment, I whispered to myself: "My parents are dead. I'm an *orphan* now."

I was unmarried and had no children. After my mother's death, my once close family had drifted apart. Our only real, remaining connection had been through our father, and now he was gone too.

I just felt so alone.

My world, as I knew it, seemed forever changed. My parents were my link to my childhood, my happiest memories, my history, and, in many ways, my sense of security. They were the longest and most constant relationships throughout my lifetime, and now, in the physical sense, they were gone.

How could I say goodbye to the ones who were the nucleus of my identity and life? My safety net? What would the world look like without them?

Now what?

I am no stranger to grief. After my mother died, I wrote *Healing After the Loss of Your Mother: A Grief & Comfort Manual*,[2] which became an Amazon Best Seller grief recovery guidebook in the categories of "Death & Bereavement," "Sociology of Death," "Love and Loss," and "Mental & Spiritual Healing." I also founded "Healing After the Loss of Your Mother – Grief Support," an online bereavement support group and sacred space for those seeking comfort and community through their loss, with approximately 25,000 members worldwide.

Through the years, I've talked with thousands who've walked through parental loss. I get this grief thing. But double parental loss felt very different.

I felt like a scared, lost child. Alone and untethered in a new world.

I had so many questions and wanted to know what to expect next. How was I going to get through this? Would the grieving process be like last time? I wanted to know the *why*—physiologically—behind what I was experiencing.

Why does our body and nervous system go so uncontrollably out of whack while grieving?

How would I move forward now? I had just said goodbye to my 50s three weeks before. Was the shock of loss triggering a midlife crisis?

I needed answers and some direction on what to do next.

I was surprised to see how few resources there are on the specific subject of double parental death, even though more than a quarter of the U.S. population—26.4 percent in 2021, per the United States Census Bureau[3]—had lost both parents.

Not one resource provided everything I needed. And few offered the kind of concise guidance a grieving, foggy mind like mine could digest. That set me out on a hunt for information through a variety of grief-related, scientific, medical, religious, and metaphysical books, articles, lectures, videos, and podcasts for answers.

I also turned to what had helped me most after my mother's death: talking to people who've been there. That included connecting with and interviewing hundreds of people from different backgrounds, ages, genders, cultures, and countries all over the world. They were all at different stages of grieving both parents, but they managed to find their way through.

These individuals included friends, distant family, fellow grievers online and in-person at bereavement support groups, as well as therapists, intuitive counselors, life coaches, and other medical and mental health professionals.

Personal experience has always been life's best teacher, and I wanted to listen to those who knew, who have traveled this path, and who could share and speak from their heart.

That journey resulted in me writing the grief recovery guidebook I so desperately needed after both my parents died.

I found answers and absorbed the wisdom that was shared with me. It felt like a privilege to have been helped in that way. I then wanted to share this collective information with other adult orphans who might be searching, hoping it helps them too.

With love and empathy, these pages are intended for anyone who has lost their parents or their parental figures, as well as for concerned individuals hoping to support a friend or loved one through this difficult time.

Navigating This Grief Recovery/ Transformational Guidebook

Because focusing and retaining information can be very difficult in the acute stages of grief, when we often need this information the most, the chapters are broken down in a focused and direct way, making it easier to mentally digest.

Since grief is not linear, this book is not intended to be read that way either. This is *your* guidebook and resource, to be used your way. You can use the detailed Contents pages at the beginning of the book to jump to the specific subject you need.

The guidebook is broken down into four distinct parts:

1. The Adult Orphan
2. Bereavement Support Community Forum
3. How to Support Someone Who Is Grieving
4. Purpose & the Path Forward

Because grief journaling is such a beneficial coping and processing method, there is a special Bonus Journaling Section at the end of the book with prompts to help gain new perspectives, take notes, and aid in promoting balance and emotional wellness.

Your Companion Through Grief

For those mourning the loss of your parents, please know *grieving is the first step in healing.*
It's a natural process if we allow it.
Knowing what to expect can help allay some of the fear of the unknown, while insights and validation from a community of compassionate others can make you feel less alone.
Those who have walked before you and share their stories can serve as guiding lights and beacons of hope.
The death of both parents is one of the most universally shared passages in life. It isn't easy, but there is a way through the darkness of grief to the light of transformation and purpose.
If you can, remember this: We don't heal *from* grief. We heal *through* it.
Let this guidebook be your grief sherpa on the journey forward. Through its pages, we will walk this road together.

PART I: THE ADULT ORPHAN

"No matter how old we are, we still need our parents, and wonder how we'll navigate life without them."

— U<small>NKNOWN</small>

CHAPTER 1

Losing Both Parents

OUR LIVES HAPPEN IN STAGES: birth, childhood, adolescence, early adulthood, midlife, late adulthood. Of the billions of people on the planet, it's usually our parents who are there with us through almost every step we take—literally and figuratively—from infancy through life's highs and lows, through every triumph and heartbreak, and each milestone along the way.

Throughout it all, our parents are the first face of love we encounter and, in the end, usually our longest relationships.

From birth, we are *tethered* to our parents on an emotional, soul level as well as a primal, physical level.

Over the course of our lifetime—if we are lucky—our parents come to embody home and belonging. They are a grounding, steady source of security in the world that follows us into adulthood, serving as our protectors, providers, cheerleaders, teachers, nurturers, and sometimes, adversaries.

When they pass from this world, we typically grieve for them and the end of a big part of our identity.

When the arc of their life is over, it marks a significant turning point in ours. Intellectually—even in childhood—we know our parents will die someday, and we expect to outlive them.

It is, after all, "the natural order" of things.

Still, few of us are ever really prepared for the hole their loss brings, nor for the scope of what else is lost and the changes they bring.

A natural rite of passage does not mitigate the initial pain of losing our primary caregivers or spare us from feeling like an abandoned child deep down. It also doesn't ease the internal and external tumult that often follows.

Losing our parents is life-altering in incalculable ways.

The expression "Home is where the heart is"[1] always had sentimental meaning for me, but my sense of home was gone after my parents passed. I felt homeless and homesick, longing for a place of safety and belonging I could never return to.

After they died, I asked myself and others: "What do I do now?" "Who am I now without my parents?" "Why do I feel so… *untethered?*"

Without our symbolic anchors, it is common to feel adrift—until we can find a way through.

Orphaned

No matter what our age or maturity, no matter how rationally prepared, self-sufficient, religious, or spiritual we believe ourselves to be, and no matter how strong or broken our relationships are, it is common to suddenly feel orphaned after our mother and father die.

After my second parent passed away, I immediately felt alone in a way I had never experienced before. I called my childhood friend, Laura, who had helped me through my mom's death eight years earlier. After I had a beat to reflect on the night of my dad's death just hours before, I said somewhat lightly to her, "I guess I'm an orphan now."

At first, I felt a little childish, even selfish when I uttered those words. It was, after all, my father who had just died. I was deeply sad he was gone, relieved he was out of pain, numb, and yet somewhat embarrassed that "I'm an orphan now" was among my first thoughts after it dawned on me that I no longer had a living parent.

I wasn't a child. I had spent six decades on the planet and was independently living my life. But the words were my raw, gut truth.

"What may be unique to parent loss, particularly in response to mother loss, is the primitive childlike emotion, among women and men, that is tied to losing this primary connection to one's childhood," writes Dr. Debra Umberson in her book, *Death of a Parent: Transition to a New Adult Identity*.[2] She confirms that the strong emotional response to losing a parent is rooted in early childhood when the fundamental attachment to a parent begins.

The death of a parent is the most shared human experience when it comes to bereavement. Not everyone will get married and lose a spouse, have children or siblings, and lose them to death. But if we live a typical lifespan, we will all lose a parent at some point in our lives.

When speaking with others who've lost both parents, I was surprised to hear the word "orphan" and terms like "adult orphan" and "midlife orphan" come up repeatedly. It was consistent across age, background, gender, marital, or family status.

It wasn't just me. And the term wasn't hyperbolic.

Identifying with the feeling of being orphaned confused many of my interviewees as well, but it seems that many mental health professionals agree that this is a real hallmark reaction in the immediate aftermath of the death of a last parent.

"The loss of both parents means one is no longer someone's child, and, in fact, one is an orphan. Psychologically, one may experience a profound sense of aloneness," writes clinical psychologist Shoba Sreenivasan, PhD, and Linda E. Weinberger, PhD, in an article for *Psychology Today*[3] regarding the complex psychological journey of becoming an orphan in adulthood.

They explain that even if the relationship with one's parents was complicated or estranged, the loss may still reverberate. Some grieve for what they lost; others grieve for what will never be.

Drs. Sreenivasan and Weinberger say that while our parents are alive, our identities as a daughter or son remain alive as well. When they are gone, we are left, at least initially, wondering about our place in the world.

What follows is an existential and often challenging period of discovery.

"Midlife orphans, orphaned adults—there's no established term for them, yet losing your parents is one of adult life's most significant rites of passage," writes Michelle Hamer in her article for *The Age*[4] about the unique grief of adult orphans. "And while society recognizes the loss that children feel when their parents die, adults are supposed to be fundamentally different, quickly dealing with the grief of losing the people that raised them from the cradle."

But grief, no matter your age, is layered and complex. It hurts. All I knew, like so many in my shoes, was the adult in us still felt like a child inside when it came to our parents' death. In the end, all I knew was "That was my *mom*" and "That was my *dad*."

It's a love and loss that cannot—should not—be minimized.

Difference Between Death of First and Second Parent

From the moment our first parent dies, it seems we not only grieve their loss, but we must try to understand and navigate this new, unfamiliar territory called grief. That often includes the first time we feel a measure of childhood loss, a disruption of the family structure, and changes to our identity and sense of safety in the world.

That is a lot to manage while we're grieving the sudden absence of one of the most important people to us. And it is true from my personal experience and from those I've interviewed that the parent we were closest to has a greater impact on our feeling of loss.

During the first loss, not only does our world change, but it's also the time we typically experience our first real brush with mortality.

Suddenly, we realize how truly fragile life really is.

And then there's the added stress of the business side of death—notifying friends and family, planning the funeral, handling the will or probate, cleaning out, and sometimes selling the family home.

Many adult children say, as I have, they feel unable to fully mourn in the wake of the loss of their first parent because they're so busy caring for the surviving parent.

One woman told me, "After my first parent died, I realized I had to grow up and show up. I was in my 40s but I had to officially become an adult. It was time to take care of the person who took care of me as a child."

Parent-child roles often begin to change after the death of the first parent, according to Dr. Alexander Levy, psychologist and author of *The Orphaned Adult*.[5] He explains that our grief can be delayed by the requirements of this newly structured relationship.

"If parents are married and living together at the time the first one dies," he says, "grief is usually considered the domain of the surviving parent. Their needs and grief take precedence." The role of adult children is typically to assist the bereaved widow or widower rather than to be the primary mourner.

"If the parents were divorced or separated," Levy adds, "the death of the first parent can mark an end to the loyalty conflicts and complicated visitation patterns that often distinguish such arrangements."

The loss of the first parent often sets up anticipatory loss for the second. We brace ourselves for the next shoe to drop. For me, I felt on edge after my mother's abrupt death, in a perpetual state of anxiety over the inevitable loss of my dad that would follow. Every phone call—especially in the early morning or late at night—sets my heart racing. This persisted for years until the day he died.

When the first parent dies, Levy explains, we begin a distinct transition into adulthood that continues until the death of the second parent. After the passing of both parents, it is as if the rest of our adulthood begins.

Levy notes that if we have two parents, we will have two different experiences with death and grief based on gender, order, and specifics of the death, as well as the nature of the relationship we had with each.

With the first parent's death, everything is new. We usually don't know what to expect or how to navigate the loss. By the time the second parent dies, we may have a sense of what is to come but still have many new questions and uncertainties.

Among those I spoke with who lost a more distant parent first, most reported that they were sad and had a period of mourning, but they were able to move forward with life fairly quickly—usually within weeks or months.

But their experience with loss didn't prepare them for the intensity of emotions that came with the death of their closer parent. It was an entirely unique experience.

For me, the loss of my mother first hit hardest. The time to recover my balance took years. When my father died eight years later, it felt like a sad relief. His situation was different. His slow decline was painful for him to endure and painful for loved ones to watch.

But what this period did afford me was more one-on-one time and the chance to get closer.

In the few years before he went to live with my sister, he became more open with me. He'd laugh more, was more thoughtful and vulnerable, and even often teared up when I had to drive home.

I remember during one of my last overnight visits, he actually said, "I love you." Three unsolicited words I waited a lifetime to hear. I will always value that much-needed "repair time."

While the death of my mother shook me to my core and took years to subside, the death of my father, though I loved him dearly, moved from sorrow and bittersweet resolve to acceptance over a period of months rather than years.

REAWAKENED GRIEF

After losing my dad, I knew I would grieve for him, but what I didn't know was it would also trigger reawakened grief over my mother's death. It was like ripping open an emotional wound, long since healed, only to feel that pain rise up again.

That's natural, according to grief experts and others I interviewed.

"A new loss will always summon up the previous one, regardless of how effectively the first loss was grieved," writes Dr. Julia Samuel, a psychotherapist who specializes in grief and author of *Grief Works: Stories of Life, Death, and Surviving.*[6]

Jane Brooks in *Midlife Orphan*,[7] adds: "Thus, the second parent's death plunges us into what can feel like a bottomless pit of emotion as we struggle with grief that had not previously been fully acknowledged."

In other words, it isn't until the second parent passes that most of us begin to grieve wholly for them both.

Personal Transformation

The impact of losing both parents in adulthood is more profound than anyone can know until they arrive at that moment.

In *The Orphaned Adult*,[8] Levy writes, "At a minimum, parental death in midlife elicits lingering feelings of loneliness, memories of former losses, unresolved conflicts, and doubts concerning life's purpose."

Throughout his years of practice, Levy noted a sudden awareness among his patients of no longer being someone's child, which carries with it a loss of childhood on a visceral level.

It is a rite of passage that includes numerous consequential losses.

For members of the eldest generation, it brings the disturbing realization that there is now no one between them and death.

Without exception, people Levy spoke with soon after the death of their second parent said, "I just realized that I am the next in line to die."

The death of our parents rearranges life as we knew it, temporarily disrupts our sense of safety and security, changes the person we once were, but inevitably shapes the person we will become moving forward.

"Family" is born from the foundation our parents (or caregivers by blood or circumstance) lay down for us, and our identities develop within the walls of this sacred structure.

As long as our parents are in this world, we remain their children. For better or worse, they anchor our sense of self and our identities.

I didn't realize what an all-encompassing psychological and emotional journey losing both parents would be, or how relentlessly it would shake up my world and drive me to re-examine so many different areas of my life.

Author Jane Brooks summarized this well after much independent research, "The more I spoke with other midlife orphans, the more similarities I detected, some subtle, others more pronounced. I found that the sense of being orphaned or abandoned is common when the last parent dies. The period after the loss becomes one of introspection and self-evaluation, as issues revolving around our family of origin rear themselves—old sibling rivalries get revived, and insecurities and uncertainties are stirred up."

My interviews with people who had lost both parents revealed a number of shared feelings and experiences, including:

- A profound sense of aloneness
- Time spent soul-searching

- Questioning one's identity
- A new search for meaning & purpose
- Recognizing the fragility of life
- Obsession over one's own mortality
- Resurrected grief over the first parent's death
- Change in family dynamics
- A need to adapt to a new world

What I found through interviews, and in various bereavement support groups, was that the absence of our mother and father becomes just as big as their presence was. And we need time to grieve them both separately.

Those who had strained relationships with one or both parents shared that they were sometimes surprised to find themselves grieving as well. Some mourned the relationship or life they did not have, others for the healing that never came.

Maybe that's why the death of our parents is so complex. It's not just about the passing of two people we care so deeply about. It also involves the passing away of parts of ourselves and life as we knew it.

And so, we begin a new passage: As our parents transition out of this life, we transition into a new one. What follows—if we allow ourselves some patience and mercy—is a period to mourn, reflect, rearrange, and redefine.

Until we arrive in that transformative place called healing.

IDENTITY

After my dad died, I didn't feel like *me* anymore. I just felt... *different*. I didn't feel like I was as nice, patient, or generally happy as I once was. I was burned out. I felt resentful toward anyone who asked me for anything because I was exhausted and had nothing else to give.

These are feelings I noticed other double-loss mourners shared.

Soon after my father's death, I revisited a wonderful counselor/energy healer who had helped me following my mom's death and validated my feelings. She said, "You *are* different. Grief and trauma rewire the brain. It changes you. It changes the way you view yourself, other people, and the world around you. Everything is just different now."

I was supposed to ask myself if the old me was really a better version of me. The people-pleaser who lacked healthy boundaries and ultimately burned myself out, told me to learn from my mistakes and heartaches and grow into a better version of myself.

She said this would naturally be a difficult time, but it could also be an opportunity to transform my life. A time to become the person I want to be and live the life I want to live.

The years of caregiving for my father, while also feeling some resentment that life was getting in the way of properly mourning my mother, dealing with my own health issues, and concentrating on my business to keeping a roof over my head, were all taking a toll.

In addition, I had taken on the responsibility for the care of a 95-year-old former neighbor who had no family in the United States. And what began as a three-month pledge to assist this difficult elder with dementia turned into a six-year-long obligation. She died exactly one month after my dad.

Like many caregivers, I was more than burned out; I barely recognized myself anymore. It was indeed time to change and rediscover who I was.

Dr. Lisa M. Shulman addresses this in her book, *Before and After Loss: A Neurologist's Perspective on Loss, Grief, and Our Brain*.[10]

"When life is interrupted by loss there is a time for grief, a time for adaptation, and then an unexpected time of choice and self-determination. It's time to open ourselves up to new possibilities, because the old ones are gone. As time passes, we can't choose if we will age, but we can choose if we will grow."

It was time.

Mortality

The issue of mortality is a subject we can no longer look away from after our parents are gone. And we must face the truth that life and death are beyond our control.

What many bereaved individuals tell me is it's not only the reality of their own death that's unsettling, but it's how they will die that concerns them. That unknown is foreboding. For others, having seen the sometimes cruelty of aging up close, there's also the undeniable fear of wasting away—both mentally and physically.

With the sound of time ticking louder and louder, and our parents no longer alive, we're officially the "older adults." As I told my friend Laura the day after my father died, "Well, looks like we're up next."

In *Death of a Parent: Transition to a New Adult Identity*, sociology professor Debra Umberson explains that recognition of our mortality can alter our outlook on life significantly. Many bereaved individuals can't avoid suddenly seeing life as short and fragile.

"The death of a parent marks a rite of passage as we make the final step into adulthood—as we lose our status of child to a parent. Stepping us closer to death, we also develop a keener sense of personal mortality after a parent dies."[11]

With this sobering realization often comes a need to deal with the practical side of mortality: It's time to get our will and affairs in order and begin scaling down our own personal and household belongings.

When we've gone through the physically and emotionally draining tasks of clearing out a parent's home and settling their estate, the importance of taking care of our own side of the street can suddenly become more pressing.

With the reality of death no longer avoidable, I, like many in this situation, began updating my will and other documents that I already had in place, but making it more turnkey in case someone had to step in tomorrow. We never know; it's not just our death we have to plan for but also the possible scenarios, where we become incapacitated in some way and unable to care for ourselves.

For the person left grieving or stepping in to help, figuring all this out on their own would be a stressful and heavy burden.

I updated my medical directives, organized a list of my passwords and monthly bills, reviewed my bank accounts, made sure all financial accounts had a named beneficiary, and set everything in a designated space with clear directions.

The National Institute on Aging[12] says being prepared can help give you some peace of mind, ensure your wishes are honored, and ease the load on your loved ones later.

If you are still in need of gathering things, it is suggested you consult legal and financial professionals to plan and prepare your:

- Last will and testament
- Durable power of attorney

- Living trust
- Living will
- Advance healthcare directive

On top of handling the business side of death, I was surprised to find how many people also felt the need to begin decluttering their own homes. It may feel like the opposite of "nesting," but it's also therapeutic, practical, and offers a productive way to channel bursts of nervous energy often experienced while grieving.

This practice is known as a "Swedish death cleaning," a morbid sounding but very positive method for organizing and clearing items in your home.

I do this several times throughout the year and always feel better after. Anything that doesn't have purpose or value goes. The things that remain take on greater value. Try to channel your own inner tidy expert, like Marie Kondo.

Rather than a grim end-of-life task, I found simplifying can free up a lot of space and energy in your home and the freshness is a welcome change.

NEW STAGE IN LIFE

Upon reflection, when it comes to our parents, there are three periods we live through:

- The innocent, childlike time when both parents are alive.
- A more complicated period after the first parent dies, and there is one surviving parent.
- A complex new world without your parents.

When I resist change, I think back on advice Cindy Bentley, a Reiki master, a former registered nurse of 37 years, and author of *Celestial Beings: How to Shift to Fifth Dimensional Living*, gave me after my mother died.

Bentley explained that when we are confronted with a lot of change—especially the unwelcome kind—moving forward means leaving our old selves and feelings of security in the world behind.

That isn't easy; it's just the way of life.

"It's okay to give yourself permission to be in pain," she said. "We need to give ourselves time to grieve that loss and adjust."

So, the questions we might ask ourselves after losing both our parents are: How will we meet this moment? Who do we want to become? What kind of life do we want to build from here?

The person we were before our parents' death is not who we are now.

Grief changes us. Moving forward—when we are ready—will bring change that can be positive and healing if we stay open and say "yes" to life.

Our greatest allies are time and the courage to believe.

CHAPTER 2

The Grieving Process

"Here we go again," I thought as I sat numb and stunned after my second parent died.

Even after surviving my first parent's death and intimately understanding the grieving process, I wasn't certain what to expect with the second loss. I didn't know whether the grieving process would follow the same path.

What I found important through my own experience and conversations with others is that gathering information early on and revisiting what worked and what didn't after your first loss can be great starter tools.

This grief recovery guidebook compiles helpful information from various books, scientific studies, different grief models, articles, and podcasts—from experts as well as everyday people who've lost both parents—to provide a guiding hand to move you from a sense of powerlessness to one of self-empowerment.

Just like love, no two losses are alike. We all grieve differently, and it's common to grieve each parent differently too. While you may encounter similar cycles in your grief, you may also find that the second death differs in intensity, complexity, and length of time.

Dr. Alan Wolfelt, the director of the Center for Loss & Life Transition,[1] created a model of "companioning" as opposed to "treating" people in grief. The goal is to walk beside someone on the journey, as opposed to attempting to fix them. This theory becomes key for success in processing a death.

Wolfelt recognized the imperative for grief to be both experienced and expressed, while addressing our new reality gradually. The bereaved must lean into the pain of the loss while focusing on self-compassion and self-care.

"Lean in." Now that takes emotional courage.

In an article about models of grief for the National Library of Medicine, Patrick Tyrrell stated that, "Wolfelt's companioning approach views grief as a natural extension of the ability to give and receive love. As such, grief is not something to avoid but should be fully experienced and even embraced in the path to healing."[2]

If we can't outrun grief, we might as well turn around and face it. And, yes, a companion in grief can make all the difference in the world. Ask any of us.

But today's culture doesn't always make it easy for the one mourning. Bereavement still isn't well understood by many, and those grieving are often not given the depth of support needed. I found this especially true when it came to the loss of our parents—as if "natural order" would minimize the impact of the loss.

Oftentimes, we are encouraged to quickly find closure and move on after the death. But it's not easy, and it's not how we heal.

Wolfelt suggests that grief is the normal, healthy process of processing the death of someone we love. If we see ourselves as active participants in our own healing, we will experience a renewed sense of meaning and purpose in life.

There is no shortcut through grief. Our best path is straight through it.

We have to feel it to heal it.

Clarifying the Stages of Grief

Many of us grew up learning about the five stages of grief, as outlined by legendary psychiatrist Dr. Elisabeth Kübler-Ross in her groundbreaking 1969 book *On Death & Dying*.[3] Her work is historically important as it began a cultural shift in the conversations about death and dying.

It's a commonly held belief that *grief* progresses in stages, but that isn't correct.

The five stages—denial, anger, bargaining, depression, and acceptance (DABDA)—were meant to describe the emotional progression of people who are confronted with illness and dying. They were never intended to describe or reflect on how a person grieves.[4]

Her final book, *On Grief & Grieving*, with collaborator and grief expert David Kessler, says, "The stages have evolved since their introduction, and they have been misunderstood over the past three decades."[5]

The book explains that the stages are merely "tools to help us frame and identify what we may be feeling. But they are not stops on some linear timeline in grief." Not everyone will experience the same emotions and there is no prescribed order to follow.

Grief doesn't happen in stages.

It might be more accurate to describe the progression through grief and grieving as fluctuating cycles; we may hit one set of feelings only to revisit them again later.

Stop, start. Rinse, repeat.

Unfortunately, there is no orderly list we can move through, check off, and be done with.

Grief is unpredictable, and as individual as we are.

No "Right" Way

Another common misperception is that there is a correct way to do grief, and many bereaved individuals fear they may be doing it all wrong. But here's the truth:

There is no right way to grieve; only your way.

I used the acronym K.I.S.S. ("Keep it simple, sweetheart") as my mantra if I felt myself becoming overwhelmed. In other words, don't take on too much and don't expect too much of yourself.

If the voice inside your head is your co-pilot through the process, be sure it's soothing, encouraging, and understanding. Be gentle with yourself. And give yourself credit: You've never lived on this planet without your parents.

You are entitled to feel sad, lost, and confused. This disorienting process is deeply personal, and entirely your own.

Four Tasks of Mourning

There are many models of grief that serve as guidelines for what an individual might experience through loss. I needed something practical and doable—a simple plan to get to the other side of pain.

J. William Worden, a professor of psychology at Harvard Medical School, proposed a practical model of grief in his book *Grief Counseling and Grief Therapy: A Handbook for the Mental Health Practitioner*[6] that resonated with me.

It broke down an otherwise intimidating grieving and recovery process into basic and bearable terms.

He divided the bereavement process into the following "Four Tasks of Mourning":

1. **Accept the reality of the loss.**
   Intellectually, you may know that your parent has died, but initially, you might be in a state of shock, denial, and disbelief. It takes time for your new reality to sink in. Denial is a temporary buffer that keeps the psyche safe until the mind can process and make sense of what has happened. Accepting the reality of death means coming to terms with the loss both emotionally and intellectually. (Acceptance does not mean you *like* this new reality; you just do not deny the death happened.)

2. **Work through the pain of grief.**
   Grief is experienced on many levels: emotionally, cognitively, physically, socially, and spiritually. This phase is about coping with the pain of grief, not avoiding it. This

stage involves naming your emotions and learning how to manage them.

3. **Adjust to life without the deceased.**
   This involves adjusting to internal, external, and sometimes spiritual changes after loss. Externally, this may mean taking on new roles and responsibilities. Family dynamics may shift; friendships may change; you may re-examine your career path or other life plans. Internally, there are adjustments to your sense of self and often existential questions about your life purpose. Spiritually, you may question your belief system and the meaning of life. As you adjust to loss, you create a new normal that, in time, balances loss with your new life structure.

4. **Maintain a connection to the deceased while moving forward with life.**
   Death does not end the emotional connection to your parents. You gradually create a balance between remembering and honoring them and living a full and meaningful life.

The Four Tasks of Mourning is a healthy, straightforward model of what to generally expect as you progress through grief. Naturally, everyone's progression will be unique to them.

As you make your way through, you may jump around between emotions and general steps, or revisit steps over again.

Whatever emotions arise, just allow them.

Growing Around Grief

Another simple theory I found works well with Worden's framework is grief counselor Dr. Lois Tonkin's popular "Growing Around Grief"[7] model.

Tonkin suggests that we do not move on from grief. Instead, we grow around it.

The following diagram illustrates the concept in a way that immediately caught my attention when I first saw it circulating in grief support groups. Many people, like me, found it instantly helpful.

People tend to believe that grief shrinks over time

What really happens is that we grow around our grief

theralphsite.com

(With permission: The Ralph Site,[8] a nonprofit for pet loss support.)

The simple visual demonstrates that in the early days after a loss, our grief may feel overwhelming and all-consuming. It may occupy every part of our mind and life, as shown above as a large black ball in a small glass container.

As time progresses, grief remains but no longer occupies such a big space. The grief appears smaller as other areas of our life grow with new experiences, relationships, memories, and joy.

"This theory suggests that there is a level of resilience that comes with a loss," explains Dr. Jenni Jacobsen, PhD, LSW, in an article for Calmerry.[9] "Even if feelings of grief remain in the foreground or rise to the surface from time to time, people learn to incorporate grief into their overall identity while finding happiness in other areas of life."

This model, along with Worden's, can reassure people with the knowledge that grief will change over time. The intense feelings and deep pain associated with early loss will not last forever.

As we adapt and change, so do our emotions and grief.

BEREAVEMENT YOUR WAY

This is new territory for all of us—we only lose our parents once in our lifetime. And while death is an inevitable part of life we can't control, we *can* take charge of the way we respond to loss, how we cope and come to terms with our grief, and how we move forward.

Understanding grief helps prepare us for the next step: the journey through it.

Just know there is hope and life again on the other side of grief. That's a promise echoed in bereavement support groups, by medical and mental health professionals, and from others who have been there.

The best you can do is to be patient with yourself, with the process, and to surround yourself with people who will have both your back and your heart.

CHAPTER 3

Empowered Grieving

GRIEF WORK VERSUS ALLOWING

SIGMUND FREUD FIRST PROPOSED THE original "grief work" theory, which involved the breaking of ties with the deceased, readjusting to a new life without them present, and building new relationships.[1]

The basic premise makes sense, except for the "breaking ties" part. I think most people in today's world have opened their hearts and minds to embrace the fact that death may end a physical life, but it doesn't have the power to end our emotional connection to the people we love.

It's the word "work" I have a problem with. Some say grief is work because "it requires the expenditure of both physical and emotional energy,"[2] according to researcher and psychiatrist Erich Lindemann, who originally coined the term based on Freud's theory in the 1940s.

For me, the thought of having to *work* on something felt like an added pressure or burden at a time when my fragile system was already overloaded, my mind fried, and my biggest triumph of the day was remembering to breathe.

When it comes to the process of grief, the reality is it happens whether we work it or not. Where there was love, there will be loss. There's no sidestepping the pain.

It's how we *respond* that matters.

It was much easier for me to think of the progression of grief as an organic process and to go with its flow. A clear intention to feel and heal is important and taking positive action to get there is key.

But rather than looking at this process as "grief work," I've found it's far more helpful to think in terms of "grief healing," where we allow a natural process to unfold.

Go With the Flow

As you begin processing your grief, remember this was your unique love, your loss. Whatever you feel is valid. Try to go with the natural current of grief, as uncomfortable as that might be at times. These feelings will ease in time.

This softer approach involves surrendering to things we cannot change. It's about being brave and vulnerable enough to accept the process.

This is about surrendering to what is… and going with the flow of life.

The Power of Surrender

For some people, the word surrender has a negative connotation, implying failure or defeat. But, in this case, it does not mean passively giving up or failing to initiate positive action.

"Surrender is the simple but profound wisdom of *yielding* to rather than *opposing* the flow of life,"[3] writes spiritual teacher Eckhart Tolle in his book *The Power of Now*.

Tolle explains that surrender is perfectly compatible with taking action and initiating change. He says, "In the surrendered state a totally different energy, a different quality, flows into your doing." He calls this "surrendered action."

"Surrender does not transform what *is*, at least not directly," he says. "Surrender transforms *you*."

Grief isn't something we can fight or rationalize away. If we ignore it, it's bound to show up down the road. So, whether it's now or later, you will need to ride through it.

Go with the natural rhythm of bereavement if you can.

At a time we might otherwise feel powerless, we do not have to be a victim of circumstance. I call this *empowered grieving*, which leads to grief healing.

As Tolle writes, "Surrender to what is. Say 'yes' to life—and see how life starts working *for* you rather than against you."

CHAPTER 4

Where to Start?

BUILD A SUPPORT SYSTEM

EXPERTS SAY THAT SOCIAL SUPPORT is a crucial element needed to help a person through the pain and loneliness associated with grief.

Our grief must be witnessed, expressed, and acknowledged. We can't just ignore it.

In her book *Grief Works,* Dr. Julia Samuel writes, "To grieve we must find a way of enduring the pain of the loss, not fighting or blocking it, and for that we need support—the love and support of our family and friends; and we need to understand what the process entails."[1]

For the bereaved, who often feel isolated, unseen, and misunderstood, many often say that having just one person who understands can help them feel less alone.

These people can even be strangers—people who connect over a shared loss and extend themselves in validating and understanding ways.

Relationship Changes

As you grieve, relationships may shift. While many connections can grow stronger, others may falter.

Some friendships may disappointingly drift away—some disappearing in the time spent caring for your parents in decline. Romantic relationships may lose balance and be put to the test. Many bereaved find it difficult to give to others at such a trying time when they can barely give to themself.

When your life is forever and fundamentally altered, it's time to focus on self-care. Others may see this as "selfish" and even become upset, but that upset usually has to do with your inability to spend as much time on *their* needs.

Maybe your role was to be "the giver," "the listener," "the steady companion," or "fun partner in crime." These people want you to "get over it" for their comfort—making your grief about them.

But don't be swayed; this moment is about you and your healing.

All that energy that had been focused outward—especially in the case of caregivers—needs to go toward rebuilding your strength and reassembling your life.

The people in your life will either adjust to the new you as you work through your grief, or they may fade away. Conditional relationships will reveal themselves. Unconditional ones will become treasured lifelines.

There are those who may not like the changes you are going through. Most of us in mourning don't like the changes either.

Some say the people you lose during the healing process are only meant to be with the unhealed version of you. That's something to think about as your inner circle rearranges itself.

I remember a friend sharing with me what her grief counselor told her, "No one gets to tell you who you are, how you feel, or what you need. Period. If they try, you can be certain they've got their own agenda."

Others in your life may have very good intentions but have their own issues and challenges and are not emotionally available. Some may not understand what grief feels like and turn away from the unpleasant subject of death.

Being so close to something so real and inevitable scares a lot of people, while others may simply lack the emotional capacity to help someone in pain.

Try to forgive anyone who isn't up to the task.

When it comes to changing relationships, nothing is more complicated as the impact a parent's death can have on a family unit, especially if the parent was the glue that held the family together.

It is sadly commonplace for our nuclear families to break down or fall apart as a result. Everyone grieves differently within a family and tensions can be high. Emotions will escalate in the wake of a loss and all it entails—from the most mundane issues to funeral arrangements and matters of inheritance.

Even though some family members may want things to stay the same, that isn't always possible, especially when existing family struggles intensify.

But if there is open communication and trust within a family unit, Dr. Samuel says, "The transition to the new reality that invariably follows a death can be weathered without the whole system fragmenting or imploding."

That's great news for many people.

Whatever the conditions, when both parents are gone, it's a stressful time of transition. It's a period where you change and hopefully grow, and you need to be around people who will support you.

As my childhood friend Laura told me after my mom died, "People who unconditionally love you will understand if you're having a hard time and not at your best right now. It won't feel this way forever. If they don't support you through this, step away."

Some people may drift out of your life. Whatever they choose, let them.

The sad thing is, if a friendship, relationship, or family unit ends, it can feel like another death.

During this time, try to make sure your circle is healthy, compassionate, and supportive.

If you find yourself without someone who can be there for you, a grief counselor or an online or local grief support group can become a place of refuge where you find comfort and support among people who understand.

GUIDANCE SHORTLIST

Having gone through the loss of a parent once before, I thought back to what helped me get through grief the first time to be better equipped for what was to come. I remembered:

- The surge of emotions will come up to be seen and felt before they can be released.
- No one can or should tell you how to mourn or when to stop.
- To be gentle with ourselves because losing a parent is a major life event.

- Pain will come in waves—sometimes tidal waves—but they will lessen over time.
- To ask for and accept help when needed.
- It took a lifetime to build memories with our parents; it will naturally take a long time to mourn their physical loss from our life.
- No one "gets over" their parents' death, but we will get through it.

Wellness Routine

Whenever I felt overwhelmed in the difficult early days after the death of each of my parents, I found it helpful to keep a short list—taped to my bedroom wall—to remind myself to do the basics of self-care each day.

It's easy to forget the fundamental things when grief consumes your mind.

If you take tasks out of your busy head and put them down on paper where you can see them, they are easier to follow. And these small actions can make a big difference in your day.

I encourage you to make a reminder list that works for you. Here's what I put up for myself—six simple rituals to start in pursuit of balance:

- Breathe deeply (Hand on heart, "I am safe.")
- Eat only healthy foods.
- Drink plenty of water.
- Rest.
- Meditation or prayer. (Three minutes to start.)
- Move body/stretch or exercise. (Three minutes to start.)

A basic wellness ritual provides gentle self-nourishment and guidance. It provides a simple structure to a temporarily upside-down world. You'll be your own supportive grief coach without having to think about it.

Permission to Fall Apart

After my father died, I re-read something I included it in my first book, *Healing After the Loss of Your Mother.*[2]

I photocopied a page from the book and posted it on my wall as another daily reminder. Feel free to do the same:

> *Early on, I remember hearing a true story in a grief support group about an older lady who came up to a woman while she was crying at her mother's grave.*
>
> *To paraphrase, the sweet stranger leaned over and gently told her:*
>
> *"People will tell you to be strong. Ignore them. You are allowed to fall apart, feel bad, and struggle because when you need to be strong again, you will be. For now, cry. Be sad. Be angry. Go ahead and fall apart because that's how you become whole again."* (pg. 10)

I love that anecdote. I read it anytime I need that feeling of support. It helps validate the crushing feelings we go through and gives healthy permission to be anything but perfect.

You have permission to grieve in any way you need to right now. It's how we heal.

CHAPTER 5

Grief Is Messy

IF THERE'S ONE THING THE bereaved may know after experiencing the death of a parent once before is that grief is complicated, unpredictable, and messy. It shakes up the snow globe of our lives and takes time for things to settle back into place.

Things change, big and small, and *change is almost guaranteed* to varying degrees with each parental loss. The shards of grief can be felt on many levels: *emotionally, physically, cognitively, socially, and spiritually.*

After going through it once, it's natural to wonder if the grief experience will be the same the second time.

The answer is: Not always.

Grief can be experienced differently between the death of the first and second parent, depending on which one we identified most closely with. The closer the relationship, the more deeply, more intensely, we may feel their loss, and the harder and longer the grieving and healing process tends to be.

If you weren't as close to your first parent who died but were more emotionally bonded to the second parent, you may be surprised by the intense emotions that arise with the second death.

And when both parents die, it can bring up entirely new feelings you may never have experienced, including that feeling of being *orphaned*.

Losing your parents is intense, no matter how old or how prepared you think you are. That's why you may experience some, or all, of the following:

What Can I Expect?

Emotional:

- You feel abandoned, like a lost child.
- You feel raw.
- Spontaneous crying if frequent.
- You can expect a roller coaster ride of emotions, including shock, numbness, sadness, anger, guilt, regret, depression, despair and more. The surge of emotions come up to be seen, felt, then released.
- You are short on patience. Even simple pleasantries may annoy you.
- You experience waves of longing and yearning.
- Mood swings are to be expected.
- Anger, early on, can be difficult to manage. Grief experts say emotions are layered. Beneath anger is pain—the pain of sadness and loss.
- The intensity of your emotions may be overwhelming and exhausting.
- It is common to feel detached, like an alien in your own body.

- You turn to magical thinking and wonder whether your thoughts, actions, and wishes could have prevented the outcome, or that your thoughts and wishes could have caused it.
- You may wonder if you'll ever feel joy again. You will.
- Your grief is all-consuming and on your mind 24/7.
- It is very common to feel like you are losing your mind. *You are not going crazy.* You are grieving.

Some may experience intrusive thoughts and images of your loved one's death or last moments. This can be unsettling, but it is not uncommon. This is your brain's way of trying to comprehend and process the experience.

You may grieve over your childhood, your family home, and the family you once were.

You may feel powerless as you process. As a result, you may try to control whatever areas of your life you feel you *can* control.

With so much uncertainty in your life, you may become more sensitive and less tolerant of people who "run late" or cancel plans. It's natural to seek reliability and consistency for a sense of security when there is little else to rely on.

Loss can overwhelm you on so many levels. First, in losing your parents, then in feeling like you're losing control of yourself.

Fleeting suicidal thoughts are also not uncommon. But if they do occur, *talk to someone or seek professional help.*

There are mornings you may wake up and feel that everything is like it was before for a few sleepy moments until you realize again, "My parents are dead." You will certainly miss the physical presence of your parents, but you will also long for the essence of who they were in your life.

Emotions may change day to day, and sometimes hour to hour, or minute to minute. There is no predictability for the process. You may be thinking you managed a particular emotion one moment, only to re-experience it again later and again and again.

While we all experience grief differently, we also *express* grief in our own ways. One person's sadness or anger may appear more pronounced; another may internalize their feelings and keep their grief to themselves. Both can be grieving just as deeply.

It's also natural to have regrets: things you wish you had said or done, as well as things you wish you hadn't said or done.

It's also common for some to suddenly let go of the things that bothered you about your parents. Old grudges or annoyances no longer matter. It's not about rose-colored glasses; it's about realizing what matters.

Grief can also bring up unfinished emotional business. This is a time of reflection and forgiveness, if you can, in time. There may be unending questions that are difficult to make sense of as your mind tries to catch up with reality. Experts assure us that it's part of processing the trauma.

You can try to cover all this pain up or temporarily soothe yourself through drugs, alcohol, shopping, or other distractions to avoid uncomfortable feelings. But be aware that this can make things worse while also delaying the healing process.

With so many unknowns, there is a constant fear of the next shoe dropping.

When we remove a parent from our emergency contact list, it brings another punch to the gut. Suddenly, saving their voicemails becomes a top priority because we never want to forget the sound of their voices and playing the messages brings them back to life in some way. We even dial their old home phone number, knowing they won't answer. Just because.

Many of us can't part with what others may not see as having "value": your mother's brush with strands of hair still in it, a half roll of mints from her purse, a nearly empty bottle of perfume. These are like time capsules. You don't need to explain its value to anyone if they are priceless to you.

No one is proud of this, but it's not uncommon to ask why your parent was taken when such bad people are walking among us. Why not them?

The loss is made harder, too, by the realization that your parents will not be present for important life moments going forward (marriages, births, milestones, and celebrations.)

Many note, with some sensitivity, the day of the week their loved one died. In the beginning, you may feel anxious and dread each time that day of the week arrives.

Finally, emotional pain can be just as debilitating as physical pain; you just don't see the cast or bandage. Both take time to mend.

This is a time to cocoon. It is natural to withdraw and go within, so you can rest, reflect, and heal.

Physical

Physical symptoms of grief can include:

- Fatigue and exhaustion
- Stress
- Headaches
- General aches and pains

- Shortness of breath
- Elevated blood pressure
- Lightheadedness
- Gastrointestinal distress, diarrhea, nausea, and stomach pain
- Change in appetite, weight loss, or weight gain
- Weakened immune system
- Sleep issues
- A low or absent libido
- Lack of coordination, clumsiness, accident-prone behavior
- Heartache

COGNITIVE

You're most likely to be preoccupied with loss when it's new. But the effects can linger for weeks, months, or longer.
These include:

- "Grief brain," also known as "brain fog," and often described as feeling "spacey"
- Difficulty focusing
- Confusion
- Forgetfulness
- Diminished information-processing
- Difficulty reading
- Endless ruminating on the topic of death
- Stunted word recall and verbal fluency
- Shortened attention span
- Difficulty multitasking

Social

Grief affects the way you interact with others. Even the most outgoing people can feel uneasy in social settings. It helps to be honest with others about how you're feeling or what you need.

It's important to meet yourself where you are and not be guided by the expectations of others.

You may feel:

- A deep need to isolate, even if you miss being around others because it takes too much energy
- Irritated by people who can't relate to loss or act uncomfortable with your grief
- Alone even in the company of others
- More social anxiety even around those closest to you
- Self-conscious being around others because you are trying to act like *the old you*
- Small talk becomes unbearable
- Unable to tolerate anything that seems petty
- A need to be more direct—even blunt
- You're more sentimental (even teary-eyed) with those you care about when you see them
- Difficulty carrying on a conversation
- Difficulty committing to plans
- Sensory overload in public and particularly sensitive to large crowds and loud noises
- Your circle of friends changing as you grow into a new you, including letting go of toxic relationships

Spiritual

For many people, a spiritual or religious re-examination may take place after the loss of one or both parents. For instance, you may:

- Question the meaning of life
- Begin to look at the world differently and change your priorities, life goals, and purpose
- Become acutely aware of the fragility and preciousness of life
- Doubt your faith or explore new ones
- Become more aware of your own mortality and the well-being of others you care about
- Grow interest in Near Death Experiences (NDE) and the afterlife—a need to know what happens when we die
- Find comfort in "signs" and dream visitations from your loved one
- Seek out new ways to possibly connect with your parents through psychics, mediums, and channelers

The first few months after loss are the hardest and you may wonder how you will survive this. But please know the intensity you feel in the beginning won't last forever.

The pain of grief will ease in time.

As grief does its thing, you just need to hold on as you work through the many adjustments it brings. It also helps to know where the emotional landmines are to prevent being spooked by them. If you can, remember to:

- Breathe deeply. It can help reset your nervous system and help calm you down

- Don't rush the process
- Try not to take on too much. It's okay to say "no" for the sake of self-care
- Resist judging your emotions or comparing yourself to others
- Let your compassionate self be your guide. When tempted to act out or behave in a way that feels questionable, ask yourself: "Is this a healthy act?"
- Resist the temptation to bury your grief. Because when you ignore it, it can show up in explosive or surprising ways later

You may find yourself wearing the "grief mask" that tells the outside world you're holding it together, while underneath you feel like you're still falling apart

And there will be moments when:

- You wish for "just one more day" with your parents, to answer questions about life and family history, offer advice, share a memory, or exchange hugs
- You may reach for the phone to call them, then realize they are not there
- It can be comforting to see their handwriting. It's a tangible piece of them they leave behind
- Wearing or touching your parents' clothes or jewelry can also make you feel close again
- You say to yourself, "I just want to feel like me again. I just want to feel normal."

The beginning is the hardest because the emotional wounds are so fresh.

Change and the unknown can feel very scary. Loss of this magnitude can be overwhelming in ways we just don't know how to process. While there is no end point to grief, the pain of grieving *will* soften with the passage of time.

In time you'll experience more good hours in the day than bad, then more good days than bad. That's how you know you're moving through it.

That's how you know you are healing.

In the meantime, give yourself grace and be patient with the process.

CHAPTER 6

How Grief Rewires the Brain

BESIDES WANTING TO KNOW WHAT I could expect after losing both parents, I really wanted to know *why* grief makes almost everyone feel so out of control. I needed to make sense of what was going on inside, *physiologically and emotionally.*

Research in brain science tells us it's not just a broken heart we are coping with in grief, it's also something akin to a broken brain.[1]

Grief temporarily rewires the brain.

EMOTIONAL TRAUMA IS BRAIN TRAUMA

There is some comfort in understanding how the brain responds and then heals following a traumatic loss. And it's true, this roller coaster ride won't last forever. Whew.

In her book *Before and After Loss*, Dr. Lisa M. Shulman, professor of neurology at the University of Maryland School of Medicine in Baltimore, writes, "Whether physical or emotional, *brain trauma is trauma.*"[2]

Grief is brain trauma.

Shulman explains that the brain interprets grief as emotional trauma or PTSD. Traumatic loss is perceived by the brain as an existential threat to its survival and defaults to protective survival and defense mechanisms.

To ensure continued existence, our brains are hardwired to respond rapidly to stress.

First, the trauma of grief triggers the primal fight-or-flight response, then the brain rapidly kicks into survival mode, releasing stress hormones (like adrenaline and cortisol) that course throughout the body. Physically, the heart races. Blood pressure and respiratory rate increase.

The sudden flood of hormones—chemical messengers in the body—sets off a chain reaction of emotional and other physical symptoms, including many we've already mentioned.

Your body's neurological rewiring activates to help you through the shock and grieving process. However, long-term or chronic stress can have a negative effect on the brain, making it harder to regulate stress responses.

I can attest to this after years in that chronic stress state. My body burned out.

It's important to remember hormonal changes triggered by traumatic loss result in emotional and physical symptoms that are *normal and necessary for healthy recovery.*

The experience of grief can be confounding, but Dr. Shulman says she hopes understanding the science behind grief can alleviate fears and restore a sense of control. I believe it does.

As she reassures us in her book, "Grieving is a protective process. It's an evolutionary adaptation to help us survive in the face of emotional trauma."[3]

In our lifetime, very few events will be more demanding on our mind, body, and soul than the death of someone we love, especially our parents.

Neuroplasticity

How exactly does "brain wiring" and "rewiring" work? Through **neuroplasticity**.[4]

Breaking it down...

Neuro: Refers to brain neurons (nerve cells), building blocks of the brain and nervous system.

Plasticity: Refers to the brain's ability to adapt and change.

Neuroplasticity is the brain's ability to modify its neuron connections and adapt its behavior based on its experiences, environment, or trauma. It is also commonly referred to as "brain plasticity."

Long-term stress and depression can disrupt the neuroplasticity needed for healing. On the other hand, stress reduction can enhance neural recovery and, therefore, our recovery.

"When we experience trauma, our brain creates connections between nerves, and it strengthens or weakens existing connections depending on the intensity of our emotional response," writes grief therapist Claire Bidwell Smith in her book *Conscious Grieving: A Transformative Approach to Healing from Loss*.[5]

The more you relive a memory—good or bad—and the more intense the memory, the stronger the neuro connection becomes. Thoughts in either direction can become your new default wiring.

In other words: "Neurons that fire together, wire together."[6]

In her book, *The Source: The Secrets of the Universe, the Science of the Brain*, Dr. Tara Swart, MD, PhD, and senior lecturer at MIT Sloan School of Management, writes, "Neuroplasticity, at its most positive, is the key to self-empowerment. It ensures that, with effort, we can overcome deeply entrenched negative behaviors and modes of thinking."[7]

Through her research, she has seen people overcome all kinds of challenges in life—including bereavement—through the power of positive neuroplasticity.

First, we need to honor and embrace the heavy feelings as we go through the darkness. That's grieving.

But in time—when we can catch our breath again—constructive reinforcement (positive neuroplasticity) of feelings and behaviors helps brighten our outlook again. We can rewire our brains in a way that leads to healing.

GRIEF BRAIN

Brain science made my brain hurt, but it explained so much of what I needed to hear and heal.

For those of us, like me, who don't "speak science," there's a simplified breakdown of this complex process. NBC News presented a short, animated video titled, "How Grief Affects Your Brain and What to Do About It"[8] that makes the concept a little more digestible.

The video explains how the impact of grief on the brain is two-fold: First, the immediate, acute pain of the loss, and then the months following as we mourn.

It demonstrates how, early in grief, the loss of someone we love functions as a major stressor, triggering the pituitary gland at the base of the brain to signal the adrenal gland to release cortisone, a stress hormone.

"Unlike, say, a temporary threat, grief is an intense, persistent stressor so your body remains flooded with cortisone that can cause your immune system to falter, making you feel run-down... even if the death of your loved one was expected, the actual event can still feel like a shock to the system," explains the narrator.

This is why we often feel numb after first learning of a death.

In the short term, a traumatized brain is bottom-heavy, meaning primitive areas of the brain, including the fear center, are overactive. That can lead to feelings of stress, anxiety, anger, and despair.

Meanwhile, the higher cortical areas of the brain (anterior cingulate cortex) are underactive. That area of the brain helps regulate emotions, affects memory, spatial orientation, and executive functions like focusing, inhibition control, and decision-making.

All this can help explain why we suddenly develop a short fuse and foggy brain, find it hard to let go of minor annoyances, cry easily, and have trouble retaining what we read.

Over time, the initial shock of loss gives way to deep sadness or depression as we continue to mourn.

"Depression can cause widespread changes across several parts of the brain, including the amygdala, which regulates sleep behavior and mood in the hippocampus which processes memory and regulates stress hormones," the video further explains.

These changes disrupt the core functions of our bodies and minds.

"Eventually, the sadness begins to lift just a little bit and then you may move on to feelings of anger or guilt, before slowly moving toward acceptance of the loss," the video concludes.
Willpower alone can't fight this process. We're not weak if we feel off. There is a scientific reason behind all of it.
Our brain is just doing what it is built to do—ensuring our survival.

NOTE: A link to the video can be found in the *Links & Helpful Resources* section at the back of the book.

Brain Healing

> *"Our brains renew themselves throughout life to an extent previously not thought possible."*
> — Michael Gazzaniga, Professor of Psychology at the UCSB and head of the SAGE Center for the Study of Mind

According to neuroscientists, researchers, and psychologists, yes, the brain really *can* restore the healthy balance between the *advanced cognitive brain* and the *primitive emotional brain*.

"Though grief can have a significant effect on the brain, these changes are temporary for most people," writes Traci Pedersen in Psych Central in an article on grief and brain healing. "The brain is *resilient* and able to rebalance itself over time, even after very painful experiences."[9]

Neuroplasticity relies on a person developing a strong mind-body connection. The negative thought patterns that occur with depression are examples of negative wiring. Exercises that promote positive neuroplasticity can then help rewrite these patterns and improve well-being.

Besides deep sorrow, chronic stress can have a negative effect on the brain, making it harder to regulate our response to stress. To promote healthy rewiring, it is recommended to strengthen parts of the brain through new, creative activities and practices.

When we learn something new, we form new pathways in the brain.

Intention will also help move you from where you are now to where you want to be. Mindful intention is a conscious aim coupled with action. This purposeful focus opens and rewires neural pathways and becomes a compass to follow toward balance again.

In the same way lifting weights repetitively at the gym builds muscles, you can exercise your brain and flex its functioning power.

The following are doctor-suggested activities that may help reverse damage and promote positive neuron firing and brain wiring to encourage healing[10]:

- Traditional counseling
- Cognitive behavioral therapy (CBT), a form of psychotherapy that focuses on modifying dysfunctional emotions, behaviors, and thoughts
- Bereavement support groups
- Journaling
- Meditation and prayer
- Mindfulness
- Exercise
- Yoga or martial arts

- Creative hobbies
- Crossword puzzles, jigsaw puzzles, and word games
- Stimulating environments like a museum or nature
- Reading
- Dancing
- Playing
- Brain aerobics—brushing your teeth with your non-dominant hand, driving a different way home, etc.

When you are ready, begin by selecting an activity that is new, challenging, and fun. Be adventurous. Commit yourself to engaging in the activity as frequently as you can.

Repetition is necessary to create new neural network connections.

Lifestyle changes also encourage neuroplasticity, such as a healthy diet (brain fuel), plenty of sleep, and exercise.

For brain healing, the goal is to drive neuroplasticity in a positive direction. If you make a wrong turn, use your inner GPS to course correct... and then keep going.

"Happy Hormone" Hack

"Among other things, neuroplasticity means that emotions such as happiness and compassion can be cultivated in much the same way that a person can learn through repetition to play golf and basketball or master a musical instrument, and that such practice changes the activity and physical aspects of specific brain areas."

— Andrew Weil, MD

As your new, positive neural pathways grow, you can expect to start feeling the "happy hormones" again.

When I felt lighter again, I wanted more because I had forgotten what it felt like to feel good.

When that moment comes for you, here are the four main "happy hormones" you'll be feeling, along with tips on how to encourage your brain to produce more of them:

- Dopamine
  Helps us feel pleasure. It is part of the brain's reward system. To produce more, be sure to: eat well, sleep, meditate or pray, exercise, be in nature, get a massage, listen to music.

- Serotonin
  Helps boost and regulate our mood and sleep. To produce more: exercise, get at least 15 minutes of sunlight every day, eat well (e.g., foods with tryptophan, which helps with mild depression and plant-based foods with amino acids). Meditation or prayer.

- Oxytocin
  Often called "the love hormone," it's produced when we bond with others. Naturally, that means if you want more, you should try things like hugs, affection, connection, petting your animals, gentle yoga, acts of kindness, sharing, etc.

- Endorphins
  Known as the brain's natural pain reliever, endorphins promote happiness, relaxation, and well-being. To boost

levels, you can: exercise, eat dark chocolate, laugh, and seek sunlight.

"These feel-good hormones promote happiness, pleasure, and positive emotions. The cool thing about them is that you have a say in when they are released," writes Tchiki Davis, PhD, for *Psychology Today*. "Whether you have a good laugh with your friend or do some exercise, your brain is releasing these feel-good hormones."[11]

And you don't even need a prescription. Just grab a piece of dark chocolate and enjoy a laugh while dancing in the sunlight with your favorite person or animal.

Who knew the key to healing and a healthy brain could be so simple?

CHAPTER 7

Grief Versus Depression

I'VE FOUND THAT ONE OF the most common concerns among those grieving is distinguishing the difference between grief and depression. When, they wonder, is it time to seek a medical or mental health professional?

Each loss brings a different kind of grief. My personal experience was very different with both parents. My mother's death resulted in more trauma than I was prepared for. In the days that followed her death, the avalanche of emotions fried my mind and body; my heart was racing, and my blood pressure was so dangerously high I had to go to the emergency room two different times.

This wasn't something I could just meditate on or pray away. I needed help badly.

My doctor prescribed anti-anxiety medication as a short-term fix, but I knew I'd ultimately have to work through my grief under my own power. I also wasn't interested in numbing or delaying the healing process.

In the heavy weeks that followed, I sought help from both traditional doctors (as in Western medicine) and holistic practitioners.

I found traditional doctors were more inclined to treat the symptoms of grief with anti-anxiety drugs and anti-depressants.

It wasn't until I went to a few holistic practitioners that I saw my grief as a natural state to process and experience.

One said, "You're not depressed. You're grieving."

I was told I'd feel depressed in grief, but that the two are different.

With my father's death, I had years to prepare, and yet still hurt deeply. I felt sad, empty, and depressed for some time, but at least I knew now what to expect and recognized the need to sit with my pain for a while.

I grieved for both my parents. Intensely, but differently.

While I had less anxiety the second time, the feeling of "aloneness" and being "orphaned" was new and a lot to process.

I took better care of myself the second time around, knowing the importance of self-compassion, a healthy daily routine, and not rushing my healing. I also didn't struggle as much.

I just went with the waves of grief, held my breath when I saw a big one coming, and learned to float.

For me, there was power in that.

Though professional help is always a good idea when you're feeling overwhelmed, it's important to understand the difference between grief and depression.

Grief is not a disease or mental disorder; it is a natural response to the death of a loved one. The grieving process is an opportunity to appropriately mourn and then heal. Normal grief resolves on its own.

Depression, on the other hand, is a clinical condition. It is a severe mood disorder and is often due to a chemical imbalance in the brain. The feelings of sadness are more constant. It can be treated with psychotherapy and/or medication.

"Grief and depression are separate experiences, but both have symptoms of extreme sadness and can affect a person mentally and physically. Someone with grief may feel like their sadness is depression, but depression can result without any external catalyst," explains Cecelia Effa in Medical News Today.[1]

Sadness is a feature of depression—they are closely tied—but not the same. Being sad is normal, healthy, and will pass; depression can have a wider, negative, and profound impact on your life.

Grief usually proceeds in unpredictable, up, down, and sometimes backsliding ways. With normal grief, most people have a period of shock, numbness, disbelief, anxiety, despair, yearning, depression, anger, and other reactions such as guilt. Gradually, these heavy feelings ease, and the person begins to feel better.

Although feelings of grief may fluctuate over time, they do not usually require medical intervention.

If symptoms don't resolve themselves, they can potentially develop into clinical depression.

According to the Mayo Clinic[2] clinical depression can range from mild, temporary episodes of sadness to more severe forms of depression, also known as "major depression" or "major depressive disorder." These are not, however, the same as grief-related feelings of depression associated with the death of a loved one.

"Though they can look the same, one difference between (grief and depression) is that depression often seems to come out of nowhere, whereas grief is a natural response to loss," writes Mary-Frances O'Connor, a neuroscientist and psychologist who directs the Grief, Loss and Social Stress (GLASS) Lab at the University of Arizona, in her book *The Grieving Brain*.[3]

She notes that "depression tends to pervade every aspect of life. People who have depression feel that almost all facets of their life are awful, rather than feeling that it is just the loss they are struggling with."

Hospice of the Red River Valley of North Dakota[4] provided information that helps explain the difference:

GRIEF

- There is an identifiable loss.
- The person's focus is on the loss.
- There is a fluctuating ability to feel pleasure.
- The closeness of others is usually comforting.
- There is the ability to feel a wide range of emotions.
- The individual may express guilt over some aspects of the loss.
- Self-esteem is usually preserved after loss and mourning.
- Thoughts of death are typically related to wanting to be reunited with their loved one.

CLINICAL DEPRESSION

- A specific loss may or may not be identified.
- The person's focus is on self.
- There is an inability to feel pleasure.
- There is prolonged functional impairment.
- Persistent isolation from others and self is common.
- Emotions are often fixed and feeling "stuck."
- The individual has generalized feelings of guilt.
- Feelings of worthlessness and self-loathing are common.
- Thoughts of death related to feeling worthless, undeserving of life, or unable to cope with pain.

Prolonged Grief Disorder

Though grief may have some common characteristics, there are, in fact, several types of grief, including Prolonged Grief Disorder, Anticipatory Grief, and Delayed Grief. Each has its own distinguishing symptoms. It's important to know what to look for, as professional support may assist in its management.

Prolonged Grief Disorder[5] is different from normal grief and depression. It involves a relentless longing for someone who has passed away.

Formerly known as Complicated Grief Disorder, it is the newest addition of its kind to the *Diagnostic and Statistical Manual of Mental Disorders (DSM)*[6] after studies over several decades suggested that many people were experiencing persistent and long-lasting difficulties associated with bereavement that were affecting many important areas of their life (including family, personal, social, and work.)

In prolonged grief, symptoms include intense yearning, obsessive thoughts about the deceased, intense emotional pain, disbelief and inability to accept the loss, detachment from the world, difficulty engaging in activities and plans, and a feeling that a part of them has died with their loved one.

Dr. O'Connor notes the upside to naming a disorder is that it lets bereaved people know that others have struggled this way too. It can be reassuring to those suffering and that treatment is available.

Traumatic Grief

Traumatic loss usually involves a sudden, violent, or unexpected death where survivors have little or no time to prepare for the loss.

"Traumatic grief tends to be more complicated than other types of grief due to its unexpected nature and many variables associated with the loss that are uncontrollable," says Alexandra Cromer, Licensed Professional Counselor.[7] Traumatic losses often bring more severe and longer durations of symptoms compared to what clinicians refer to as uncomplicated grief or bereavement. Traumatic grief, says Cromer, tends to last at least a year or longer, depending upon a person's resources, resilience, and access to professional help.

ANTICIPATORY GRIEF

Anticipatory grief—also known as anticipatory mourning—is defined as the grief before a loss. This can happen when dealing with a loved one who has a terminal illness, or, for example, one is enduring the long slide associated with Alzheimer's disease.

A person dealing with anticipatory grief begins the grieving process long before the actual death occurs. For many, it often starts just after the diagnosis. But knowing death is looming can also provide precious time to resolve any issues from the past, become an opportunity to grow closer, ask questions about family, learn more about your parent, and say goodbye.

One aspect of anticipatory grief I experienced was how lonely it can feel in a world that often doesn't acknowledge a significant loss until the person has passed away. I was grieving the loss of so much as my father's disease progressed.

"Despite time to prepare for a death, research has shown that anticipatory grief is accompanied by intense anger, loss of emotional control, and atypical grief responses. These responses may be due to the uncertainty and loss of control brought on by anticipatory grief," writes Dr. Cynthia Vinney, PhD, in Verywell Mind.[8]

There can be a lot of anxiety while a person is steadying themselves for a loved one's passing. Watching them deteriorate and suffer is unbearable. "As a result, we lose our sense of safety and security, leading to a range of stressful emotions that may not be felt after a loss has occurred."

There's a constant fight-or-flight state of hyper-vigilance, whether it's waiting for the phone to ring with bad news or just the energy required of us as caregivers.

"These things (and others) can contribute to a sense of relief when the death eventually comes, and a guilt that can come with that relief. These feelings are common and totally normal when someone has experienced an anticipated death,"[9] writes Litsa Williams for What's Your Grief.

She reassures us the feeling of relief in no way diminishes our love for the person we have lost. "It doesn't, of course, but this relief can be a confusing feeling. We sometimes need to consciously remind ourselves that the relief does not change the deep love we had for the person, rather it is a natural reaction to the illness."[10]

Other professionals, such as Dr. Vinney, cite a variety of factors when estimating how long this type of grief might last—including the age of the deceased and the loved one at the time of the loss, the length of time in anticipation of the loss, personal traits, and circumstances.

Delayed Grief

Sometimes, a person may compartmentalize a death and put off the grieving process for a later time. This often happens when someone is under too much stress, needs more time to process the death, or doesn't want to go through all the heavy emotions associated with grief in the moment.

Others wait until something triggers the need to process their feelings. Some people do this intentionally, some unintentionally.

"In some cases, a person may feel a need to 'put on a brave face' and 'be strong'," says Angela Morrow, RN, in Verywell Health. "Or they might feel a responsibility to help other loved ones cope. The pressure to take on this role may start during the funeral arrangements or in the week and months that follow."[11]

SUICIDAL THOUGHTS

Those in severe emotional pain—especially immediately after a loss—frequently say they feel they "have nothing to live for" without the parents they loved. They just want to be with them again.

These feelings are understandable. The struggle is heartbreaking and very real. I also experienced these feelings after the loss of my mom.

In most cases, it's not that the person wants to die; it's that they want relief from hopelessness and despair. It's sometimes impossible to imagine how you could ever be happy again.

While suicidal thoughts are not uncommon, grief experts say these emotions are usually fleeting.

"Suicide is a permanent solution to a temporary problem" is true. There's no undoing it.

It's important to remember that grief changes with time. It really does. Many people who have experienced suicidal thoughts have also expressed relief that they didn't make an irreversible decision when they were at a low point.

But pulling out of an emotional nose-dive isn't easy. It takes time, support, and sometimes baby steps.

It's important to note that if someone has been depressed before the loss or has had thoughts of suicide in the past, they may be at risk of having suicidal thoughts while grieving.

It's not unusual to consider or express thoughts of suicide after the loss of your parents. Taking it a step further and imagining how to do it, planning, or starting to give your possessions away in anticipation of ending your life, however, is a red flag that signals the need for immediate help.

Remember that emotions fluctuate wildly as you grieve. The profound pain you may feel one moment may pass in the next. "This too shall pass" is particularly true when it comes to grief.

If suicidal thoughts become more than fleeting in time or intensity—or you find yourself seriously thinking about harming yourself in any other way—please talk to someone. It often helps to vocalize your pain with a friend or someone who understands.

It can help release those feelings of hopelessness and despair.

If there's no one to talk to and you live in the United States, please reach out via phone or text to 988,[12] the new Suicide & Crisis Lifeline, to connect with trained mental health professionals.

The 988 lifeline will connect callers either way to the existing network of more than 200 local crisis call centers around the country. The National Suicide Prevention Lifeline's 10-digit number, 1-800-273-8255 (1-800-273-TALK), will remain active, but calls will be routed to 988.

The National Suicide Prevention Lifeline provides FREE and confidential emotional support to people in suicidal crisis or emotional distress 24 hours a day, 7 days a week.

If you are outside the United States, please visit the International Association for Suicide Prevention site at www.Iasp.info.

A doctor, mental health professional, your place of worship, or regularly attending a bereavement support group can also be valuable, nonjudgmental lifelines.

No one can do this kind of pain alone. And no one should.

When to Seek Help

After my mom died, I asked Lisa McGahey Veglahn, Senior Vice President for Education, Hospice Foundation of America, how to know when it might be time to seek professional help with grief.

She said grief is often compared, as we've said, to a roller coaster ride, with highs and lows that are dramatic in the beginning but eventually level off.

She said if emotions aren't evening out as time passes, or if they are getting more intense or disrupting your life (not eating, bathing, being able to work or function), then professional assistance can help.

Anyone prone to depression, anxiety disorders, or personality disorders should also consider professional counseling. If the loss was unexpected, traumatic, or you lack family or social support or had a strong dependence on the deceased in life, you might also want to talk to a mental health professional.

A little preventative care can keep things from spiraling.[13]

Working with a therapist can also be useful for identifying coping strategies and working through complex emotions, whether you are in acute grief or just trying to regain balance in your life.

When in doubt, consult your physician, grief counselor, or mental health practitioner to determine what's best for you, your mind, and your body.

DEPRESSION AS YOUR ALLY

When I was going through this a second time, I thought back to something I read in *On Grief & Grieving*.[14] that explained the important role depression plays in the grieving process. It really helped me.

The book details how normal feelings of depression that come with grief are seen by our society as something that needs to be fixed, noting, "Of course, clinical depression that is left untreated can lead to a worsening of one's mental state. But in grief, depression is a way for nature to keep us protected by shutting down the nervous system so we can adapt to something we feel we can't handle."

According to Kübler-Ross and Kessler, "When you allow yourself to experience depression, it will leave as soon as it has served its purpose in your loss. As you grow stronger, it may return from time to time, but that is how grief works."

It's true; sometimes the pain is there to help us heal. Lean into that.

CHAPTER 8

How Long Will This Pain Last?

THE TWO QUESTIONS I HEAR most from those who've just suffered a loss are "What can I expect?" and "How long will this pain last?"

During a time with so much uncertainty, it is understandable to want to know when the hurting will end. Direct answers would be nice.

But different kinds of grief (normal or uncomplicated grief, prolonged grief, traumatic anticipatory grief, and delayed grief) have varied timelines even if they run similar courses.

Those with complicated grief may, naturally, need more support to help move through their emotions. For them, the timelines tend to be longer and can vary widely.

In "normal" grief, everyone's process is still different. As mentioned previously, a person's emotional makeup, the circumstances surrounding the death, your relationship with the deceased, your support system, and your natural coping mechanisms all factor in.

Grieving is not a one-size-fits-all journey.

Throughout healing, grief might feel more like cycles on repeat (or what I call the déjà vu of grief) rather than a linear path. Just try to go through the bumpy moments without judgment, knowing it's all moving you forward.

The First Three Months

For most people experiencing normal, uncomplicated grief, the shocking early days after a death are obviously the most difficult.

In the first three months, you cry a lot, if not every day. Nerves are tattered. Anything can trigger your emotions, and you may not have the energy to do the basics like getting out of bed, showering, eating, cooking, doing simple errands, or going to work.

Socializing is painful. You may want to be alone and curl up in a ball. That's okay. Crying in the shower or in your car often becomes a daily ritual. Screaming in your car, like many do, becomes a form of primal therapy.

Letting yourself cry and isolate for a while is perfectly natural. In fact, it's enormously healing. It releases a lot of trapped, sad energy that builds up in your body.

In the first few weeks, time seems to operate in a twilight zone. There are notification calls to make, an obituary to sometimes write, a funeral or memorial to plan and get through, thank-you cards to get out, documents to gather, wills and estate matters to tackle, and more.

The business of death can feel never-ending.

As far as bereavement leave and the opportunity to mourn are concerned, in the United States, the Fair Labor Standards Act (FLSA)[1] does not require employers to offer bereavement leave. However, most employers offer three days off, and more "generous" policies might include up to five days off. (Be sure to talk to your company's human resources department to get specifics about your employer's bereavement policy.)

No one can emotionally process grief in 3-5 days.

In the first few months, you are just settling into the reality that your loved one is gone. You've now made it through the whirlwind of the days following the death and funeral, but it's also when the condolence cards and calls start fading.

I don't think most people realize the amount of grieving that continues long after the rest of the world has "gone on." That's when you may really need a little extra support.

The quiet can be deafening.

If you do need anything, it's important to ask and to be specific. Most people are uncertain of how to help when it comes to grief. The fact that they may say nothing doesn't mean they don't care. It usually means they don't know what to do.

When you reach out, the people who care about you will be glad you did.

In the first few months (to a year), try not to make any important life-altering decisions, especially regarding finances, career, moves, or relationships. Because you might be a little impulsive and reactive due to grief brain, it is recommended to wait until your emotions are settled and your mind is less foggy.

That includes not pushing yourself too soon to clean out your parents' personal things or the house. Going through your parents' personal belongings is something you want to take your time with. When you do go, invite a friend, take a lot of tissues, and allow the memories to come up.

If done in a gentle way, you can make it a very cathartic experience despite the sadness.

If you can clean out in stages, that's best.

Keep in mind that you can always box or store items for later if there are reasons you must clear things out sooner rather than later. But give yourself room to decide what you want to keep in the family, what you want to pass on to others, and what to give to charity.

Three to Six Months

Things become a little easier in this period. The pain is less acute but still intense, and you may find more moments of peace.

Slowly, you begin to take deeper breaths. Getting out of bed becomes easier, but you may still be introspective and somewhat distant from others. Socializing takes energy, and your battery may still be low.

You'll laugh again, and you may feel some guilt about that. Or it could be months before you find moments of happiness. But you will get there. It might start with noticing the color of the sky or hearing the sounds of nature or the city. You realize again there is life going on around you. And you are a part of it.

On the outside, you may look closer to your normal self again, but on the inside, you're still working through many emotions and still have a way to go.

But note, above all, that you are still standing.

Six Months to a Year

Each month of the first year ticks off the calendar like a minor achievement. Other times, those months can feel like hash marks on a prison wall.

Most people say at some point between the first six months to a year, instead of simply observing the world around them, they begin to re-engage with it again.

And as you make it through a year of "firsts" without your loved ones, birthdays, holidays, anniversaries, special occasions—the sadness may be revisited again.

There are many adjustments during the first year. You will feel the absence of your mother and father again and again.

This is why you need to go easy on yourself. Just when the wound starts to heal, suddenly it's opened again.

I grew up mistakenly thinking there was a year of mourning out of respect after someone died, then it was over, and it was back to life as usual.

Oh, was I wrong.

I had no idea what grief really was, how complex it could be, or what it entailed until I went through it myself. When you've made it to this point, consider it something to be proud of.

You've been hurt, but you got back up, you kept going, and you have endured.

The First Year & Beyond

You may find some relief as the second year rolls around. Grief becomes more manageable. As you become more aware of how different things are, it will still be painful, but not as extreme as that first year.

Still, others have found that the second year was harder as things quieted down and the weight of this new reality settles in. The people you loved are gone and not coming back.

Now you really feel it.

For those who were especially close to, or dependent on, their parents, year three can still be challenging. It takes quite a mental shift to acclimate to a loss like this.

We're all so different. Most people going through grief agree that it takes at least a full year or two, sometimes more, just to feel somewhat normal again.

Long-Term Adjustments

In many ways, grief never completely goes away. I didn't realize that when I lost my first parent.

Why doesn't grief end? Purely because where there is love, there will be feelings of loss. There will always be a part of you that will miss them.

"Tu Me Manques."

While the sorrow may always be there just below the surface, love will always be there too. In all ways. That's how the human heart works.

I still experience days when sadness hits out of nowhere. Holidays and birthdays still sting on occasion.

But there is more joy again now. I can look at photographs of my parents and not cry. A sweet memory can bring a smile to my face instead of a tear to my eye. A story about my parents that I've never heard before can fill my heart with surprising happiness.

Those are all such gifts.

Life is different, but my parents are still very much with me and part of my life. Long-term adjustment involves acknowledging that shards of grief will always be there, and nonetheless, we continue to move forward into our new world.

Your New Normal

I've never met anyone who is ever the same or whoever truly gets over the loss of their parents. While it may change you, your family entity, and your world, you learn to adapt.

Creating a "new normal" involves balancing grief and loss with the joy of everyday life.

It's rebuilding your life after loss. In time, you will find a new you, a new way forward, and enjoy new experiences and dreams—just without the physical presence of your parents.

You will live again. And when you do, you will bring your parents with you, still feeling your connection and keeping them a part of your life in your own unique way.

CHAPTER 9

Grief Triggers & Glimmers

TRIGGERS

WHETHER YOU ARE AT THE point where you are moving forward in your grief or it's early on, grief triggers will be a natural and inevitable, sometimes dreaded, part of the grieving process.

Triggers are moments of reawakened grief that take us by surprise and remind us of the person we lost. They can happen anywhere and at any time. They are especially frequent in the early days after a death.

Some triggers may be obvious and predictable—like a change of season, a familiar scent, the holidays, birthdays, Mother's and Father's Day, passing their favorite restaurant, cooking their favorite dish, attending a funeral, or certain songs that remind you of the person you miss.

Other triggers may be unexpected and catch you off guard, setting you off balance.

Triggers can be big or small. It can be helpful to note what makes you particularly emotional so that you can normalize your experiences and know what to expect.

I was shopping at the grocery store soon after my mom's death, for example, and got emotional when I saw a bottle of classic Bosco syrup on the shelf.

That simple item brought up memories of the chocolate milk my mother would make for me as a child. It seems so insignificant, but the emotions were right there on the surface. *I missed my mom.*

Barely able to breathe, I abandoned my cart and burst into tears when I got back into my car. Over chocolate milk.

"These triggers spark intense emotions and memories associated with our loss. They can catch us off guard, causing waves of sadness, anger, or anxiety. However, understanding and managing these grief triggers is an essential part of the healing process,"[1] writes Laura Presutti, MEd, EdS, LMSW, and Founder of River Oaks Psychology, a group of independent-practicing mental health clinicians that provide online services.

"The impacts can vary from person to person," she says, "but grief triggers often give rise to a range of emotions such as sadness, anger, guilt, longing, or anxiety. They may bring back memories of the loss and remind us of the void left behind."

Triggers can leave us feeling vulnerable and emotionally fragile, but they are perfectly normal and common among all of us grieving.

Even years and decades down the road triggers may still occur, but in general they lose their potency. While they may be uncomfortable, try to remember… they are there as remnants of your love.

Glimmers

A "glimmer" is the opposite of a trigger. Glimmers are those micro-moments that spark feelings of joy. They are especially welcome when you need hope the most.

Have you ever stopped to admire a beautiful sunset? Relished a great bite of food? Admired the colors of a vibrant rainbow? Stopped on a walk to smell fragrant flowers in bloom? Delighted in the warmth and taste of your favorite morning coffee on a rainy morning? Melted into a tender hug or smiled at a photograph that captured a happy moment?

If so, you've experienced a glimmer.

Deb Dana, LCSW, first coined the term glimmers in her 2018 book, *The Polyvagal Theory in Therapy: Engaging the Rhythm of Regulation*.[2] Glimmers occur when we experience brief moments of happiness that allow our nervous system to feel safe and calm.

"If you paused to notice the pleasure you were experiencing and to savor the moment, then your mental health and nervous system automatically benefited. Learning to find glimmers helps to enhance well-being and reduce stress," according to the Newport Institute, a mental health and substance abuse treatment center.[3]

Relish these moments. Don't let them pass you by. Write them down. Take a mental snapshot. Refer back to them if you need a boost or just want to remind yourself what you have to be grateful for.

According to clinical professionals, noticing and appreciating glimmers can help build emotional resilience and develop a less overactive nervous system over the long term. They help put you into a state of regulation, connection, and safety more often, because you have more neural connections that are programmed for ease and relaxation.[4]

What's a good sign you've focused on a glimmer? When you get the tickly, warm, and fuzzy feeling in your gut or your heart swells with positive emotions.

The more you practice looking for glimmers, the more you'll find them. If you can, set an intention to bring them into your life.

Then, stay open.

If you catch yourself running on autopilot, slow down. Look around. Take in your surroundings and look for the glimmers. Just the other morning, I filled my dog Sage's food bowl, and my little kitty, Rumi, butted in and pushed her canine sister aside for the first few bites.

Rumi is small but surprisingly assertive. And she enjoys sampling everyone's food.

It was a comical sight to see, but I turned away to continue what I was doing in the kitchen.

Then I stopped.

I turned back and really took this endearing moment in, letting myself feel all the warm and fuzzies over this cute sight. I listened to her purr while she ate. I noticed the soft, pretty fur on her back and lingered in the glimmer.

The other day I was running errands and heading for the post office when I stopped and looked up at the sky. I noticed the colors and the soft white clouds drifting by and watched the palm trees swaying in the warm breeze.

Looking out into the distance, I could see and feel the serenity of the blue ocean. Over the noise of people and cars in the parking lot, I heard birds chirp. I took a deep breath and felt the warm and fuzzies rise.

I stayed in the glimmer for a few minutes, appreciating how good it felt in my body and recording the feeling in my mind.

I lingered in the glimmer.

Be sure to use all five senses when you notice glimmers—your vision, hearing, taste, smell, and touch. This is a form of mindfulness that also helps to calm and settle you. Keep a list of these magic moments so that you can experience them again.

There's a whole wide, beautiful world going on around us that we sometimes fail to notice. When we are in the depth of grief, it barely registers.

So, stay in the glimmer when you can. It's free and it's fun.

CHAPTER 10

Holidays & Special Occasions

HOLIDAYS, BIRTHDAYS, ANNIVERSARIES, AND SPECIAL occasions are happy events for most people, but when you are grieving, they can be especially difficult.

Unless a person has buried someone they love, it may be impossible for them to imagine why these special dates are so hard without them. It can be an isolating feeling for many.

When you lose your parents, these once happily anticipated dates—previously filled with childhood memories, treasured traditions, and nostalgic feelings—become colored by your grief.

We don't just mourn their loss; we mourn the way things used to be.

Special dates on the calendar—ripe ground for grief triggers—are especially challenging during the first year following your loss. Your raw year of "firsts" becomes reminders, again, that our parents aren't here with you.

When two key pieces of the family puzzle are gone, the final image just doesn't fit or look the same anymore.

Plan Ahead

In addition to the complicated feelings associated with particularly special dates and anniversaries themselves, there's often anxiety in the days leading up to each special day. The grief resurfaces and our nervous anticipation escalates. It's hard to gauge what to expect or how we'll feel when the day comes. And while we can sidestep the most obvious triggers (sad songs, certain places, etc.), it's impossible to avoid specific dates on the calendar.

Knowing these days may bring some emotional uncertainty, it's helpful to plan in advance, so you can spend your day in a way you'll like. As you plan, give yourself several options, with several escape routes in case your feelings change. Because they often will.

You may surprise yourself and feel great the day of the celebrations, or you may feel like climbing under the covers and staying there. I think it's true that misery loves company, but grief loves isolation.

There are times when you just need to be alone and skip a special day entirely.

Again, plan for different scenarios to give yourself options and the freedom to choose.

Relieving Pressure

One way to make dates easier for yourself is by letting go of expectations. The reality is things will not be the same now that your loved ones are gone, so try not to hold to an impossible standard.

Be compassionate with yourself.

If you know a particular day will be hard, tell your family and friends how you are feeling and that you might not be up for attending events right now. It's okay. Just be honest with them; they can't help you if they don't understand what you are feeling.

Just know, if it doesn't feel right for you, it isn't right. No need for explanation or justification. You can revisit things again next year... Remember, this is your life, your grief. Respecting your own feelings—whatever and wherever they are at any point—is self-care.

Like my childhood friend, Laura, told me, "Don't feel obligated to do *anything*. It's just another day on the calendar."

If you find yourself doing anything out of a sense of obligation rather than enjoyment, consider letting it go. At least for now.

You can always find your own way to honor your loved one and also honor your grief.

FAMILY TRADITIONS

It's your choice if you want to stick with old family traditions or build new ones. You may find that creating new traditions lets you look forward to a fresh way of doing things—ways that don't carry memories of the past or bring a sting of sadness with them.

My family used to do big, elaborate Thanksgiving gatherings with turkey, all the trimmings, and so much more. It was a big food fest, a lot of laughs, and a lot of work.

Now that my family has branched off in different directions, I prefer either an intimate dinner out or a small potluck with friends, board games, music, and holiday movies.

This has become my new holiday normal. But the traditional big white box of See's Candies continues. It always evokes good memories of my grandma's house and all those fun-filled, big family gatherings from childhood.

Change doesn't have to bring sorrow. The happy parts can come with you.

Continuing with any family tradition—either in part or in whole—helps give a sense of continuity and belonging. Traditions are important because they are a part of your history and who you are. In sharing any tradition with others, you can keep the good memories going, help others know you better, and bring your lost loved ones into your present celebration.

Family traditions help demonstrate that even as things change, some can endure.

New Customs

Of course you'll miss your parents; the symbolic empty chairs are always there. But you can continue to honor them through new customs and in other heartfelt ways.

This can include cooking their "famous" recipe, baking or bringing their favorite dessert, playing their favorite music, lighting a remembrance candle, or sharing funny stories.

One grief support group member shared that she started a new custom of saying grace before a holiday meal as a way of including her late parents in the celebration.

She said, "I wasn't raised in a religious household, but I've started doing this at family functions. It's a way to show gratitude, include my parents in the gathering, speak their name out loud, and acknowledge that even though they are gone, they are still very much a part of our family."

Introducing new customs that honor your parents is an excellent way to show your love and keep your relationship alive.

THE HOLIDAY SEASON

The holiday season is a particularly difficult time of year. It usually starts in September as the weather starts to change, the autumn leaves start turning color, the air feels crisper, and the nights become shorter.

Things then begin to hit harder when seasonal decorations start going up.

Grief can be tough to deal with at any time, but it's extra challenging during the "home for the holidays" season.

If you don't feel like you can handle the holidays, perhaps you can take a vacation instead this year, go to the movies, or stay home and order take-out.

Some people choose to celebrate a week or so before the actual holiday to avoid the expected triggers and chaos of the outside world. This way, they are able to enjoy some of the season but on more manageable terms.

If you choose to attend celebrations, you can let people know in advance that you are having a hard time and may need to cut it short. Allow yourself a social off-ramp.

With so much stress built into the holiday season, you don't need to put any added pressure on yourself.

To help minimize any holiday-related anxiety, you might consider avoiding the malls or large crowds or just be sure to do your gift-buying well before the holidays if it feels like it's too much for you. Shopping early in the day during the holidays when it's quieter or buying your groceries well in advance of a major holiday can help as well.

Ordering gifts or groceries online is also an immense help if you're looking to avoid the mad rush of shoppers and any potential triggers.

But some may look forward to the holidays after their own season of grief. This traditional time of year can bring some normalcy and comfort to those who are able to embrace it. A return "home" can sometimes be just what you need.

Consider what makes you comfortable and know that you have many options available to you. There's no wrong choice. What matters is what feels right to you. For now.

Mother's & Father's Day

The first Mother's or Father's Day without your parents is the hardest and most bittersweet for most everyone. It's especially difficult when your loss is fresh and there is more yearning than joy to the day.

"I dread Mother's Day and Father's Day. I don't feel like anyone understands what these holidays mean to those of us who have no one to celebrate with," said one grieving individual, summing it up for many.

I remember when my first Mother's Day without my mom was approaching.

I was prepared to feel sad that day. I wasn't prepared for the blitz of television commercials for flowers and gifts, promotional emails, Facebook reminders, and the grocery stores filled with cards and so much commercialism weeks in advance.

On the day of, just hearing someone in public say, "Happy Mother's Day," was enough to bring me to tears. It has gotten easier through the years; now it's just another day. If you can, try to release expectations of what this day "should" look like. If it makes you feel good to honor your parents on these holidays, then follow your heart. If it's just too painful to deal with, that's okay too. You don't have to observe it.

It can get complicated for those with children who want to celebrate you, or a mother-in-law or father-in-law who are still alive and need to be acknowledged. If you can't just ignore the day, it helps to let others know that you are grieving, and this holiday is hitting too close to home this year, and hopefully next year will be different.

It can be helpful to avoid social media during these holidays. Facebook, Instagram, and other sites will be flooded with pictures and stories of people with their mother or father, enjoying the day, and those images can be painful reminders of what you've lost.

You can be happy for others who still have their parents while still feeling a twinge of jealousy and sadness that you do not.

How you feel about the day may change over the years. If grief is anything, it's unpredictable. Meet yourself where you are on the day and give yourself permission to celebrate or not. You might feel the build-up was the worst part. Stay open.

I try to focus on the fact that I show my love for my mother and father all the time; I don't reserve it for the one day Hallmark has designated as special.

Your Birthday

Most people I've interviewed say their birthdays just aren't the same, especially after their closest parent dies.

"I know I'm a grown adult, but it was my mum and dad who only really cared and made an effort on my birthday. My mum would get me a cake and balloons and remember all the little things. With that special love gone, it just doesn't feel like a celebration anymore," said one support group member.

For many, it's a parent who'd be on the other end of the first phone call of the day, singing "Happy Birthday," sending a card and a gift, and making a fuss over you. They were the ones who usually went out of their way to show how special you were on your big day.

When those calls and cards stop coming, birthdays can feel a little empty, even if you have wonderful people in your life. Once again, if you don't feel like celebrating, this is perfectly okay.

My first birthday felt like someone took all the air out of my balloon. All the "happy" in "birthday" was gone. This is a very common feeling among us.

I didn't want to acknowledge my birthday at all the first year. By the second, I didn't want to feel bad again and decided to make my birthday more about my mom and appreciate the fact she gave me life. I tried to make my birthday a reminder of the joy *she* always felt on the day.

I do try to enjoy them at least a little now. It's been a day I prefer to spend alone, but I'll buy myself a gift, make myself breakfast in bed with flowers on a nice serving tray, and treat myself to a massage or facial.

I take good care of the daughter my mom loved so much. *Loves. That love doesn't end.*

Each year forward gets a little easier. Happy memories do have a way of finding their way back into your mind and heart.

Their Birthdays

The day your mother and father were born will always be *their* special day.

While the absence of a parent may feel heightened as their birthday nears, there's some comfort in a continued connection and keeping their memory alive. You may think back on past birthdays, how old they'd be today, or how you might be celebrating if they were here.

My mom's first birthday hit me hard because she loved birthdays, which made me miss her all over again. My dad was not very sentimental, so acknowledging his birthday was less emotionally complicated.

Whether you choose to acknowledge the day with some kind of celebration—or in quiet reflection—is up to you. Many who've just lost a parent feel compelled to do something, no matter how big or small, to continue the celebration of their life. After all, you've been celebrating their birthday every year of your life, and just hitting the breaks can feel jarring.

Some people find comfort in gathering with other family members or friends, perhaps going to their favorite restaurant, baking their favorite birthday cake together, or sharing happy stories.

It is a nice feeling to see how your parents can still bring people together.

For more private ways to spend the day, you can also volunteer in their name or do an activity they enjoyed. Perhaps plant a tree or something in the garden, something you can watch flourish and visit as it grows.

While we may not celebrate the day formally anymore, it is still a special day that's noted in our hearts.

The Anniversaries of Their Death

This is a tough one for all of us. There is so much build-up, especially the first year, and it has a way of bringing up everything you've lost all over again. It also feels like an important milestone in recognizing *all you've come through.*

I woke up the morning of my mother's death anniversary and thought, "How did I survive all that?" I heard my mom say in my head, *"You didn't give up, Honey. You didn't give up."*

Neither have you.

These anniversary dates are, again, really no more than a date on a calendar and hold no more power over us that we are willing to give them. Like many other milestone days, most find the anticipation far worse than the day itself.

Just for the first year, I wanted to do something special. My mom was a world-class hugger and loved her garden. I chose to plant an almond tree (she loved almonds) in my backyard that I called "my hugging tree." As it grows and its roots get stronger, it reminds me that I'm growing and getting stronger too.

More importantly, it's a comforting way to pay tribute to her and think about her in a good way every day, not just one day of the year.

Whatever you choose—be it a formal recognition, a private moment, or nothing at all—do whatever will bring your heart some peace.

CHAPTER 11

Keeping Your Relationship Alive

"Death ends a life, not a relationship. All the love you created is still there. All the memories are still there. You live on—in the hearts of everyone you have touched and nurtured while you were here."

— MORRIE SCHWARTZ
(FROM THE BOOK *TUESDAYS WITH MORRIE*)

I *FEEL THAT QUOTE BY* author Mitch Albom from his book, *Tuesdays with Morrie*. *"Death ends a life, not a relationship."* When I was at my lowest, I'd put my hand on my heart, take a deep breath, and repeat that sentence.

After each of my parents' death, I ached for their physical presence. One more hug, one more walk, or one lazy afternoon just watching a movie together…

But I knew, without any doubt, their physical death would not end our emotional connection. A parent's love is forever. So is mine. I learned to focus on nourishing our bond—that eternal tether. I wasn't going to break that.

I keep my parents alive through my memories. I share stories about them and have planted a memory garden for my dad with his favorite flowers near "the hugging tree" in my yard.

My backyard is my sacred space, a place I can go to regroup, take in the beauty of the flowers for peace, and hug the almond hugging tree for strength and connection. It feels like a literal embrace from heaven and a physical extension of my mom and dad.

Gradually, you can create your own balance between remembering your parents who are gone and keeping them alive in the present moment.

Talk to Them

When I asked people in various bereavement support groups what they do to keep their bond with their parents alive, the number one answer was "talking to them in my head."

That's my favorite way to feel connected too.

Why does it feel so good? Because it keeps them alive. It brings them to you in the present moment.

One group member said, "I talk to my mom every day. I wish her to be well and happy, tell her what signs I've seen that I feel she's sent. I just talk."

Another said, "I talk to my dad and ask him to guide and protect me. Sometimes I'll cook my mom's recipes and ask her to walk me through them. I feel their spirit constantly! I feel thankful and blessed!"

Still, another said that when she needs her mother, she asks her what to do and then waits for the answer. "I still let her mother me."

If our parents have been in our lives, even for far too short a time, we know their voice. So, we can probably imagine what they'd say in any situation. If we ask, then listen... it's possible to still "hear" them.

I like to talk to whichever parent I want to connect with on walks while cooking, gardening, driving, doing things around the house, or just commenting about something throughout the day.

I loved cooking with my mom and still do. I use her cookware and that makes me feel like we're in the kitchen together. The other day, I was making egg salad. Nothing exciting, I know, but my mother would always seem to put her own spin on a recipe.

As I was stirring everything in a bowl, I heard her voice in my head telling me to add raisins. My mom loved to play in the kitchen. Out loud, I said, *"Raisins? In egg salad? Lady, you're crazy!"*

I googled raisins and hard-boiled eggs, and up popped "Curried egg salad." Curry was a mom-favorite ingredient I don't really care for. She put it in everything. I took a moment to read all the ingredients and said out loud, *"Oooh, gross... she'd probably love it,"* then I could hear her *lauuuugh.*

I felt her with me, still making the mundane fun.

Bring Them with You

Simply thinking about your parents and bringing them with you in moments of solitude can help you feel less alone.

One grief support group member shared, "I talk to my parents every day, and I do things that we used to enjoy together, like picnicking, gardening, watching a favorite movie, or cooking a favorite meal… I imagine them enjoying these moments with me—through me. It keeps me connected to them and I don't feel so alone. I actually enjoy these activities with them in this way, and also take in each experience more."

I've done this too. When I walk barefoot on the sand by the ocean, I imagine my mom in spirit, enjoying what she loved so much in life through me.

Storytelling

Sharing stories about your parents—and especially hearing new ones from others—provides comfort like few other things can. It not only keeps their memory alive, but it also brings *them* to life in the present moment.

We tend to talk a lot about our loved ones right after they have passed. I know I started to feel a little self-conscious about this, but then a friend—who had never met either one of my parents—said, "Don't stop talking about them. That way, we get to know them better."

Another friend told me, "Keep sharing. It's your birthright." Wow did that feel good—encouragement to share my heart, without judging my love or my grief. That's big.

I would often talk about my parents when they were alive, so it felt odd to just stop mentioning them after their passing or worrying about oversharing while mourning and adjusting.

Here's the deal: Your parents are *still* a part of who you are. If reliving happy memories feels good, keep talking about them.

It's healing. People get to know you better when you share and more deeply understand what you've lost. Listening to stories about your parents and hearing their names spoken can feel good. Encourage people to share.

Stories can help you maintain a connection to your parents and help you honor the life they lived. They will always matter, so keep sharing.

Present Tense

People often use the past tense when referring to those who have passed. If someone asks what your mother or father's name *was*, try to gently correct them and use the present tense. "My mother's name *is* Irma." "My father's name *is* Dennis."

Their names do not die with them.

They feel more alive to me when I speak this way as well. Their names remain, and it feels empowering to show their presence still in my life.

The essence of who they are in my life remains. They always will.

Irma *is* still my mother. Dennis *is* still my father.

I *am* still their daughter.

Neither time nor death can take that or our connection away.

Journaling

Writing your thoughts down on paper can sometimes feel like a direct line of communication to your mom or dad. It can move your emotions from your head and body onto paper and be cathartic.

It's another favorite way those I've interviewed say helps keep the parent/adult child relationship alive and present. It's also a powerful go-to for processing grief.

When your parents are no longer here to talk to, sharing through journaling can feel like a real conversation in the here and now.

You can write down all the things you'd tell them about if they were still here: happy news, a problem you're having, gossip, events of the day—anything.

Another grief support group member told me that talking to her parents through journaling keeps her parents close. She wasn't ready for their relationship to end, and she realized it didn't have to.

"I will have some sort of relationship with my parents for the rest of my life," she wisely said, "because I will love them for the rest of my life."

Death doesn't have to win.

Memory Boxes

Memory boxes are another popular way to keep your connection alive. Find a box—any kind of box—wooden, even a shoebox, and decorate it in your own way. Then, fill the box with keepsakes, photographs, and favorite small items that remind you of them, such as jewelry, a driver's license, or keepsakes that mattered to them. You can also include cards with their handwriting on them.

In doing so, you'll have a part of them that you can still see and touch.

Anything that reminds you of your parents and brings back happy memories can go in that box.

BE OF SERVICE

Many people told me they felt closer to their parents by becoming involved in an interest that was important to their parents—like a cause or charity they championed. In doing so, the children carried the torch on their parents' behalf, honoring their parents' service and reaffirming that their lives continued to matter.

MEMORIAL TATTOOS

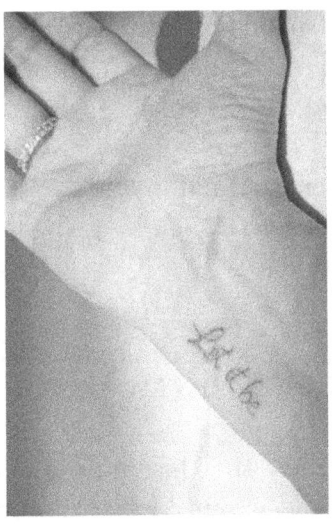

I went 52 years without a tattoo—until my mom died. I've been surprised, though, to see how many people get a remembrance tattoo as a way to honor a parent who died. I liked the permanent, committed nature of an honor tattoo to externally express grief.

A tattoo can also help people maintain a bond with the deceased. Getting a tattoo of a parent's handwriting is common and a daily reminder that the parent is with you.

My tattoo inscribes the words "Let it be" on my inner right wrist. I was inspired by the story of how Paul McCartney came to write that classic song. The backstory is that in the late '60s, McCartney's mother, Mary (not the biblical Mary), who died when he was 14 years old, came to him in a vivid dream to comfort and console him as he was going through a very difficult time.

He said he saw his mother clearly, particularly her eyes, as she spoke those simple words of wisdom: "Let it be." Her message was to be gentle, don't fight things, just try and go with the flow and it will all work out.

When he woke up, he felt it was a magical moment where he was actually able to spend time with her again. I've had visitation dreams, and they are *very different* from ordinary dreams; they are remarkably vivid and very real.

When I am low or troubled about something, I brush my hand across my memorial tattoo and can hear my mom softly say, "It's going to be okay, Honey. It's going to be okay."

She's always with me.

STEPPING INTO THE PARENTAL VOID

Grief involves a lot more than just missing someone. On a physical level, we grieve our parents' loss. On an emotional level, we grieve the loss of who they were, the role they played in our life, and, if we were fortunate, how they made us feel: loved, protected, special.

If your relationships were close, your parents sponsored that energy for you when they were here. They held that space. When they are gone, you feel the absence. In time, you can fill the emptiness by building their best qualities inside yourself.

A part of healing is learning to step inside the void that is left behind.

When something is broken around my house and needs repair, I think of what my "Mr. Fix-it" dad would do and ask him to guide me as I use his tools. If I listen, it does feel like we're doing it together.

Be resourceful, I remind myself. I *am* my father's daughter.

My mom, for her part, was a fierce protector. I sometimes think about what she would do in certain uncomfortable situations and channel my inner-Irma by being more like her.

I can be strong, I remind myself. I *am* my mother's daughter.

My mother was also a nurturer. She still encourages me to always love and nurture myself. When I follow her example, I feel her presence.

When we merge some of our parents' best qualities inside ourselves, we recognize how much they *remain* a part of who we are, and everything we are growing into.

There are so many ways we can continue to feel our parents in our lives and keep those relationships alive.

Our connection never has to end, if we continue to breathe life into it, strengthening the bond between this world and the next.

I've heard it said that "Grief is just love with nowhere to go" (by Jamie Anderson). The sentiment feels accurate and understandable when we are grieving, but I think it can be elevated a step.

I'd rather think that the love beneath grief *does* have a place to go. When we keep our relationship with our parents active and alive, it becomes a dynamic, living connection.

When nourished, love is a continuing bond that even death cannot end.

CHAPTER 12

The Afterlife

"We are not human beings having a spiritual experience. We are spiritual beings having a human experience."

— Pierre Teilhard de Chardin

"What happens when we die?" This is one of life's greatest mysteries and one of the questions I hear asked most often among the bereaved. The majority of people want to believe the spirit lives on after our mortal life ends, that our loved ones are safe, and that we'll see them again.

The afterlife—or life after death—is described as the belief that an individual's soul consciousness survives and continues on after physical death and is common to the majority of the world's religions.[1]

Missing our deceased loved ones leads many to not only seek answers to this age-old question but also search for new ways to connect. This may include opening our minds and asking for signs, synchronicities, visitation dreams, or—unless it is rejected by specific religious or personal beliefs—seeking consultations with reputable psychics, mediums, or channelers.

The thought that there is an afterlife, that our consciousness lives on, offers solace for many.

When I asked a diverse group of bereavement support members their thoughts about the afterlife, there was an overwhelming response of hopefulness.

One member said, "I know we can never be sure about what's next, but I hold on to the hope that there is an afterlife. That belief keeps me going. I think God, or whoever you believe in, gives us signs as encouragement, to help us feel the connection to our loved ones who've passed, and a way to show us this isn't over."

Another shared, "I am a Christian and believer in heaven and the promise of an afterlife. My faith in God and Jesus sustains me through my grief. It gives me hope that we'll all be reunited again."

"I am of Bahá'í faith and believe the soul progresses even after death," offered another, adding, "That brings me a lot of peace."

Still, another group member commented, "I am not religious. I base my beliefs on the fact that the Universe is energy, which can never be destroyed. It can only change state. My parents no longer have a physical body, but their energy is still here, perhaps in a more powerful form now."

But the one that seemed to sum up the feelings of so many came from the member who said: "The idea of an afterlife gives me tremendous comfort. I am obsessed with learning everything I can about near-death experiences (NDEs) and what's on the other side, about signs and the departed coming through to us in our dreams. I know there's more. I have to believe that our love transcends all realms."

While some who define themselves as atheist don't believe in God or an afterlife, and others who identify as agnostic and don't believe it's possible to know if there is a God or life after death, the vast majority I interviewed were hopeful that the spirit does live on.

After the death of their parents, many people begin a hopeful quest for proof of "life after life."

Crossing Over

A compelling glimpse into "the other side of the veil," the figurative reference to the barrier between heaven and earth, comes from Dolores Cannon, a world-renowned hypnotherapist, speaker, author, and creator of the innovative Quantum Healing Hypnosis Technique, focusing on past life regression and historical research over a nearly 50-year career.

Cannon says her unique hypnosis technique enables her to take clients back through time—from this lifetime through former lives—accessing their subconscious minds and the higher mind that connects with universal wisdom.

Cannon gathered information about the death and afterlife experience of hundreds of clients, including memories of their own deaths, as well as crossing over into the spirit realm and beyond.

These reports were consistent in detail regardless of cultural and religious backgrounds. Through years of work, Cannon was able to weave the story of the interconnected nature of life, death, and all soul beings.

Cannon's extensive research revealed how many view death not as the end but as the natural, blissful doorway to the next phase, a new beginning in the eternal odyssey of our soul's consciousness.

Based on her research, Cannon says, "Life after death is guaranteed for all of us because the soul is indestructible."

And there is nothing to fear.

Throughout her past life regressions with clients, Cannon found reassurance that no one is ever alone after dying. We are *all* helped through the transition from life through death and beyond by loved ones on the other side—our guardian angels or ethereal beings of light.

"Accepting death should be as easy as embracing life, because one cannot exist without the other. The spirit is not just a thing that resides in a body; it is eternal energy, created by Source,"[2] she contends.

In a 2008 lecture on "Between Death and Life" for the Ozark Mountain Transformation Conference,[3] Cannon detailed how clients described the process of death during their sessions. In general, this is what they communicated: First, as the person is dying, the soul pops out of the body and their consciousness floats above, looking down. There is no pain, and many are surprised by what they see below.

After leaving the body, the soul is drawn through a tunnel of bright white light that some call God or Source Energy. It is the tunnel that separates the physical and spiritual worlds.

All are given a chance to go back, but the radiant love is so indescribable, so incredibly powerful, that few want to return. "They want to go on... they want to go home," Cannon said. "It's the ones who are left behind who grieve about it."[4]

Understanding a soul's purpose as complete is something mortal loved ones may never fully comprehend. This is especially true in the case of unexpected passings.

When death comes, the silver cord that connects the physical and spiritual body throughout our life is severed and the spark of life is gone.

Cannon says there is no pain in death; it is a moment of profound liberation. The "physical dead" feel *free*. It is described as being as quick and painless, like "getting up out of one chair and sitting down in another."

Once we cross to the other side, the soul finds a place more beautiful, peaceful, and colorfully vibrant than anything we could have ever imagined here on Earth. It's described as the energy of pure, unconditional love. We can also appear healthy again and at any age we choose, not like the body left behind.

Even your beloved animals who've passed will be there to greet you.

That side of the veil, they say, feels like the true reality and home. When we wake up there, we look at this life with confusion, realizing it was just a temporary, lucid-like dream.

Many reportedly say, *"But it felt so real."*

After crossing over, there is a period of orientation, and during a life review, we come to understand and *feel* how we affected others in our lifetime—in both good ways and bad—and see how we are all interconnected.

When their sessions with Cannon were over, most reported their fear of dying was gone, and there was a new peace for those who had lost loved ones, concluding that death is not the end.

NEAR-DEATH EXPERIENCES

People who have reported near-death experiences share similar observations as described in Dolores Cannon's work. The difference is these subjects don't sever the silver cord between the physical and spiritual bodies. Instead, they return to life from the tunnel of white light.

Reports of near-death experiences seem to captivate our collective imagination and offer hope that there may truly be life after death. These vivid and highly detailed stories have stretched across cultures and human history.

Whether these accounts provide evidence of the existence of the afterlife, it seems binge-watching documentaries, television series, videos, or devouring books about near-death experiences and the afterlife is a common, healthy obsession after losing someone close.

We want to believe.

Near-death experiences are personal accounts from people who have nearly died or were clinically dead and then brought back to life. They have been documented by religious believers and non-believers, by the skeptical, by neuroscientists, physicians, and agnostics. Even those who've been blind since childhood have been able to describe out-of-body experiences and "the other side" in near-death circumstances.

This unique phenomenon has been reported by people of all ages and from countries throughout the world.[5]

One interviewee shared with me, "I have become completely preoccupied with information on the afterlife. I can't get enough of reading or watching videos about NDEs. I have always believed, but now I crave for it to be real."

Another woman told me, "Reading and understanding about near-death experiences has helped me tremendously after the death of my parents. I also had a friend who went through her own near-death experience. It changed her. She was an atheist but now believes there is a heaven, and it is most likely the next stage of consciousness. She no longer fears death and now believes that our bodies may die, but our spirit lives on in a different energy form."

Still, another had an up-close look at this phenomenon from the experience of their spouse, "My husband never believed in an afterlife prior to that experience. Now, not only does he believe, but he feels that he was brought back to life for a purpose. Hearing him share his experience with me and all the videos I've been watching have brought me so much comfort since losing my parents."

While no two NDEs are the same, most of the recorded accounts do share broad similarities: The person's heart temporarily ceases to function at some point prior to recovery; they become pain-free and detached from the body in an out-of-body experience, allowing their consciousness to observe their physical surroundings from a point above the room.

They travel through a tunnel toward a bright "divine" light of "magnificent love" and encounter deceased loved ones and angelic beings. They describe a life in review process where they relive events from the point of view of others, feeling both the pain and joy they caused. Everything in review happens in what feels like the blink of an eye, and the person experiencing the near-death experience is given a choice to return to their earthly life—although most do not want to leave the pure unconditional love they are enveloped in.

The term "near-death experience" was coined in 1975 by Raymond Moody, MD, PhD, considered to be the "father" of the modern NDE movement. His pioneering book *Life After Life* is the groundbreaking study of people who experienced "clinical death," were revived, and who tell, in their own words, what lies beyond death.[6]

A former agnostic and skeptic known for his extensive research and numerous books into the afterlife and near-death experiences, Moody shared his personal conclusions about his decades of research findings into NDEs in an interview with the Intuition Network.[7]

"I don't mind saying that after talking with over a thousand people who have had these experiences... it has given me great confidence that **there is a life after death**. As a matter of fact," said Moody, "I have absolutely no doubt, on the basis of what my patients have told me, that they did get a glimpse of the beyond."

Moody later participated in the 2011 documentary *Afterlife*,[8] an exploration into the question of "What happens when we die?" that included a series of compelling first-hand accounts with survivors of near-death experiences, as well the participation of fellow NDE expert Jeffrey Long, MD, author of *Evidence of the Afterlife* and founder of the Near-Death Experience Research Foundation. Long's foundation is the largest NDE research database in the world, with over 1,600 accounts of near-death experiences from around the globe..

The overwhelming conclusion? Death is not the end. Millions of people through the ages report being transformed after their near-death experience. Most claim they are left firmly believing in an afterlife and report considerably positive shifts in their attitude, beliefs, and values.

Often, according to Dr. Moody, people who make this journey back to life stop chasing whatever they were focused on before—like power, fame or money—and become more spiritual, compassionate, or altruistic with no further fear of death.

Those who return are also left with a profound personal understanding that consciousness is not confined to the physical brain. It is an enduring force that transcends physical existence.

The most significant transformation he observed was the belief that the most important thing we can do while we are alive on earth is to learn to love.

VISITATION DREAMS

Who hasn't wanted to hug someone who they've lost just one more time? Through visitation dreams, many feel like they really have. I've experienced these kinds of dreams and *they feel very vivid and very, very real.*

Visitation dreams also feel vastly different than normal dreams. Typically, you will be left with the knowledge you have really communicated with your loved one.

For those who believe that the deceased can and do visit us in our dreams, these "visitation dreams" can fill us with tremendous comfort.

In addition to feeling genuinely real, visitation dreams also characteristically:

- Exceptionally vivid, and you will remember these dreams with great clarity upon waking up and for years, if not for the rest of your life
- Present the deceased as healthy and happy and appearing at any age
- Often come with a loving and peaceful message or purpose
- Feature fine, clear details
- Feel like a real-life visit, as if the deceased is alive again and standing with you
- Soothing but short in duration

"A visitation dream is not a creation from your subconscious mind. Visitation dreams are when a non-physical being communicates with you while you are sleeping," says Melanie Beckler, author, meditation guide, and founder of Ask-Angels.com.[9]

She explains that souls communicate while we're sleeping because our ego mind doesn't block communication at this time. It's then much easier for them to get past the filters of our mind, the filters that keep us focused in the physical, and as a result, block activity from the spiritual realms.

I remember the first dream I had of my mom after she died, and it left me with such an incredible feeling. In the lucid dream, I could see someone who looked like my mother walking toward me on a tree-lined path. As she came closer, I did a double take in disbelief. I couldn't believe my mom was alive; we had just held her memorial service.

As she stepped nearer, I stared closer and saw her cute nose, the distinct color of her eyes, her smile. *That was my mother... she was alive!*

I said, "Mom! I thought you were dead." She appeared radiant and happy. She said, "No, I'm very much alive. See, I'm right here." She smiled and wrapped her arms around me. *It was as real as our last big hug.* "I am not imagining this," I thought.

"I have to tell everyone," I told her. But she didn't want to worry them; they were already adjusting to the idea that she was gone. She wanted to spare them any sadness over her leaving again.

The dream wasn't long, but I felt her love, reassurance, and support from beyond the physical.

Beckler adds, "Dream visitations offer proof that even after death, souls live on and through dreams; they have a way to communicate with their loved ones still alive in the physical."

SIGNS

> *"Those who don't believe in magic will never find it."*
> — ROALD DAHL

A peacock, my mom's favorite, appeared by her Quan Yin, Goddess of compassion & mercy statue in my yard just after she died.

Many say the body is temporary, but the living soul is forever. I like to think that when the soul leaves this world, a part of their energy stays behind in the hearts of those they loved here on earth. A bond is a bond, and love is an eternal, unbreakable energy.

I personally believe it is only the body that dies, not our connection on the level of spirit. Our souls remain intertwined forever.

So, those who have passed never really leave our side.

Many believe the deceased can still communicate with us and send "messages of love" to show us that they are still with us. These special signs are like "winks" from above that offer comfort, smiles, reassurance, and a sense of their continued presence.

For many drowning in grief, they can also feel like lifelines to establish a connection to the one they miss.

I asked my friend Brent Atwater, medical intuitive, animal medium, and author of *Lessons from Loved Ones in Heaven: How to Connect with your Loved One on the Other Side to Heal from Loss*, to help explain the physics behind how signs and synchronicities work.

According to Atwater, "Connection with Spirit is based on electromagnetic energy exchanges. It's based on pure energy, yours on earth and theirs on the other side. It's that magical connection of the fibers of your heart's energy interwoven with their eternal *living* energy through love."[10]

"Signs are how spirits subtlety starts the process of revealing to you they are a continuing and integral part of your daily routine," she says. Atwater told me that asking for and believing in signs will reweave new energy threads between life and death across dimensions.

If you doubt a sign, she suggests thinking about the last time something like that happened. Coincidence? Ask your loved one to do it again; she says they do listen.

"If you don't believe in yourself, trust in and allow Spirit to do their part. The more you practice, the more responsive they will be."

In her book *Signs: The Secret Language of the Universe,* author and psychic medium Laura Lynne Jackson writes, "Our teams on the Other Side are ready and eager for us to acknowledge this connection. Yes, they send us signs and they're very good at it, but they still need us to engage with them to expand the possibilities of communications by creating new symbols of meaning—and strengthening the cords of light between us."[11]

Co-creating with the other side can be an adventure. Jackson says when we ask for signs and acknowledge when they appear, two things happen: You'll find getting signs becomes easier, and it will bring joy to your life and to those on the other side. These signs can include certain animals like red cardinals, blue jays, hummingbirds, butterflies, and dragonflies.

Other signs that may indicate loved ones are near include rainbows, a feather, coins, a favorite or meaningful song, sensing their presence or smelling their familiar fragrance, lights flickering or sudden electronic malfunctions, heart symbols, goosebumps, or random (literal) signs with a message that feels tailored just for you.

The possibilities are endless.

Talk to your parents in your head; I believe they can hear you. Ask to feel their presence; you might feel tingles or chills. Ask for signs that will let you know it is them. Ask them to visit you in your dreams.

I ask for signs all the time and when I acknowledge and delight in them, they seem to come more often.

Find the unique ways your loved ones communicate with you. My mother, for example, speaks to me a lot through songs, and they always seem to come at just the right moment.

During these moments, I know it's her, but I still wonder: "Was that me thinking of her, so she sent it, or was it her thinking of me and I received it?"

Hmmm. I like it either way.

"Three Little Birds" by Bob Marley and the Wailers came on in the hours after her memorial and still comes on, perfectly timed, when needed. The first four lines of the lyrics, about positivity in the face of adversity, is so her (and she called her daughters her three little birds). Marvin Gaye's "Ain't No Mountain High Enough" is another one I know she uses to speak to me. The timing is always uncanny.

Signs will often show up for you in ways that are unmistakably your loved one. I never stop asking for signs, and I'm told it's never too late to start.

My mother's favorite bird is the peacock. I had lived in my house in Southern California for 18 years when she died, and I hadn't seen a peacock in my yard once, although they do live in a nearby city. The week after she died, a peacock appeared in my front garden for the first time. It stood, with its beautiful feathers, almost posing in front of my mom's Quan Yin statue I had placed there.

From then on, peacocks became our sign. They have shown up at my back door welcome mat, resting like a dog to make me laugh. I have found them lounging on my back deck sectional couch, and a few have been so comfortable that they just stroll through an open door unannounced.

And every year since my mom died, a peacock—and sometimes her babies—appears in my yard on Mother's Day. *Every* year. They are more common in my neighborhood now, but I know it's her with a wink, a nod, and a playful giggle.

When my dad passed, it took a few months for the signs to start. I was feeling a little dejected because it felt like he just disappeared, so I asked him to please send a sign that he was okay and still with me.

I asked for something that I couldn't brush off as a coincidence. Four days later, I was enjoying my morning coffee and looked out my front glass French doors to see a cotton-tail bunny hop by, pause, look around, then hop away. *What?*

That was undeniably from my dad! We used to take my dog to a grassy park by his house, and we'd sit on the bench in the early mornings or late afternoons, watch the bunnies, and relax. The "bunny park" was our special place.

In the two decades now living in my home, I've never seen a rabbit in my yard or the surrounding neighborhood. Ever.

If you ask yourself, "Is that a sign?" Trust that it is and ask them to keep coming.

Synchronicity

While some events in our life can be considered random, others can feel like direct orchestration from the Universe.

The term *synchronicity* was coined by Carl Jung—the famous Swiss psychiatrist—to describe "a meaningful coincidence of two or more events where something other than the probability of chance is involved."[12]

They are unexpected events that seem related but are not explained by conventional reasoning. For many, these symbolic occurrences are believed to be a form of after-death communication (also known as ADC).

Have you ever thought about someone and then received a text from them out of the blue? Or dreamt about a casual friend and ran into them shortly after? Have you ever driven through a crowded parking lot only to have a prime space open up—seemingly just for you? Noticed repetitive symbols that have special meaning to you, like your birth month and the day you were born? Or, without prior planning, find yourself in the right place at just the right time?

These may feel like mere coincidence to some, but for others, it's the Universe and your loved ones coming together to send you messages that get your attention.

My first true synchronistic experience was almost beyond my imagination.

A year after my mother died, I settled down for breakfast and decided, out of the blue, to finally use her dishes and vintage coffee serving ware. It made me feel like we were enjoying a relaxing morning together again.

I was thinking fondly back on the times she'd stay with me, and while I made breakfast, she'd run down to the corner convenience store to surprise me with the Sunday *L.A. Times* and fresh-brewed coffee. She often did thoughtful things like that, and those were happy memories.

I had canceled my newspaper subscription years earlier, but I always loved that Sunday ritual.

So, imagine my surprise to find—*somehow*—what was waiting outside my gate a short time after I poured the coffee from her carafe. A fresh copy of that day's Sunday *L.A. Times*.

I kid you not. She *was* there with me.

Later that same morning, I went for a walk by the ocean with my dog; something I'd also do with my mom when she visited. A woman who looked *exactly* like my mom walked toward me. I didn't just stop cold and stare, my dog stopped and whimpered like she recognized her Grammy.

I couldn't help but get choked up and fight back tears. It felt like she was magically put in front of us. I wanted to hug the stranger, but I didn't want to freak her out.

The woman wore the same white long-sleeved shirt, the same black walking pants with white stripes, and the same visor my mom would wear in the summer months. She also donned similar tennis shoes, styled her hair at the same length and color, and walked with the same slight slant and gait.

I took a photograph of the woman in the white shirt who was walking with her friends to show others who knew my mom. Without saying anything, I asked who they thought that was a picture of, and everyone assumed it was an earlier photograph of my mother.

Not only did I feel like I really had morning coffee with my mom, but she also still managed to bring the Sunday paper and got the rush of "seeing" her in the flesh again. It is an amazing feeling to be in *sync* with those we love on the other side.

I look at these not as "coincidences" but as beautifully orchestrated "cooperative incidents." Signs and synchronicities are all around us, just waiting for us to notice.

And once we do, we cannot deny their magic.

My Mom with her grand dog, 12/25/15

CHAPTER 13

Coping Tools, Tips & Strategies

*"When we learn how to become resilient, we
learn how to embrace the beautifully broad
spectrum of the human experience."*

— JAEDA DEWALT

MOVING THROUGH THE GRIEVING PROCESS is not simple. It can be exhausting to our mental, physical, and spiritual bodies.

In the beginning, you may need a pause from your normal routine to acclimatize to what has happened. Allow yourself the time you need to sit in the landscape of loss.

As the days and weeks go by, and you feel yourself growing stronger, you may want to find ways to bring some restorative balance back into your life.

Now is the moment for gentle self-compassion and care.

This is an important time to focus on being your own best caregiver, while developing coping strategies and mindful practices that help you process your feelings and nourish your body.

Consider this chapter your "grief first aid kit" for everyday use and to keep it handy in case of emergencies.

See what suggestions work best for you. Small changes can make a big difference when consistently applied over time.

The intention to feel better can help you move forward in positive and constructive ways.

When your world feels out of control, these tools can help regain a sense of balance and put structure back into your life in ways that will, hopefully, soothe your mind, body, and soul.

MIND

> *"Set peace of mind as your highest goal and organize your life around it."*
> — BRIAN TRACY

One of the most common fears while grieving is that you might literally be *losing your mind*—not just "off," but seriously broken.

Most often what you are experiencing is temporary. That fact is worth repeating again and again. Complicated, seemingly irrational feelings are perfectly natural in grief.

After the death of someone loved, the surge of grief can easily overwhelm us, leaving us feeling out of control. It's not uncommon to feel disconnected from who we are and from our own thoughts and emotions.

Although we can't control the outside world, we *can* learn to control our inside world.

This takes self-compassion and patience.

What you give your attention to is a choice. At first, you may just feel swept along in negative or numb default mode, but with practice, you can learn to move your emotions in a positive direction.

This may not be easy while in acute grief—when heartache may be all-consuming—but in time, you can learn to refocus so that you, not grief, are in charge.

In the beginning, let these three simple words be your "path to healing" mantra:

Honor. Feel. Heal.

Softly remind yourself to:

- **Honor** whatever feelings come up.
- **Feel** your feelings, even the unpleasant ones. They are coming up to be acknowledged and released.
- **Heal.** Rebuilding our lives through loss is what we are reaching for so we can live fully again.

Gentle Self-Talk

Calming, reassuring self-talk is critically important.

Keep reminding yourself you are doing the best you can. You will have good days and not-so-good days. Forgive yourself if you don't know how to "get it right." *There is no right.* It may be temporarily chaotic, and that's to be expected.

Grieving is not easy. For most, if not all, of us.

Hopefully, you won't be confronted by a negative friend who judges your way of grieving. Please don't do it to yourself.

If there's a negative tape playing in your head, press stop. Then toss that old tape out.

Soft, nurturing self-talk can go a long way in soothing yourself through difficult days. Remember to be your own best supportive friend with your inner dialogue.

Cry

Some people associate depression with crying during grief. Experts say crying can be a sign of healing. Tears are your body's natural release valve for stress, sorrow, anxiety, and frustration.

Tears are cleansing and a way to purge pent-up emotions that otherwise build up in your body.

"To stay healthy and release stress, I encourage my patients to cry. For both men and women, tears are a sign of courage, strength, and authenticity," writes psychiatrist and best-selling author Judith Orloff, MD in *Psychology Today*.[1]

"Crying makes us feel better, even when a problem persists. In addition to physical detoxification, emotional tears heal the heart."

She writes that tears are usually just below the surface when we are grieving, but some may worry that if they start, they might not be able to stop. According to her, if a person is depressed, it can be a sign they are holding back.

There's nothing to apologize for or feel self-conscious about. Tears help us move through—and honor—our pain.

Primal screams

Loss is a primal pain. When your heart is screaming on the inside, screaming out loud is not only a way to express and release your grief, but it's also potentially cathartic.

Some people use their car or a spot in nature far away from others as their private refuge and sacred space to scream, sob, yell, swear, and let out pent-up, intense feelings without anyone around to judge them.

Psychotherapist Zoe Aston, in an article for *Well+Good* said, "Screaming creates a chemical reaction that is similar to the one you get when you exercise—you get a dopamine hit and some endorphins going."[2] (She also notes it helps to release the stress hormone cortisol.)

If screaming doesn't feel right, even loud, breathy exhales or grunts can help to "stay connected to the body while accessing where stagnant energy is stored," says Aston.

WRITING & JOURNALING

Journaling has long been recognized as a transformative physical and psychological instrument in grief recovery and personal growth. It may seem repetitive to mention it again, but experts say it's among the most powerful tools in processing the complex emotions associated with grief.

A journal helps take the burdensome thoughts, reflections, and intense feelings experienced while grieving out of your head and put them on paper where you can better name, understand, and process them.

Writing or journaling can also be used to express feelings of guilt or resentment that still linger and need to be released. (If it's composed in letter form, you can write down your thoughts, read them aloud, and then burn the letter to release your feelings.)

Keeping a journal—whether in a ringed notebook, a notebook pad, or a fancy leather binder—can help you notice patterns in your grieving and identify areas where you could use support.

A journal is for your eyes only, where you can explore your innermost thoughts without fear of judgment. It is written in a way that encourages an unvarnished stream of consciousness writing.

You are encouraged to write with a pen or pencil to allow your brain to be more engaged and increase your focus.

Expressing sadness, guilt, anger, or confusion can help individuals acknowledge and release these emotions, leading to a sense of relief and emotional catharsis.

Many use their journal to share news of the day with their parents, just like when they were here.

Over time, your journal becomes the story of your grief journey, where you can track your progress and gain a new perspective that ultimately leads to healing and personal growth.

STOP. PIVOT. POINT.

It is important to give yourself permission to feel whatever you are feeling: The good, the bad, and the ugly. When feelings come up to be seen, processed, and then released, you are proceeding in a healthy, albeit sometimes uncomfortable, way.

If feelings become stuck in compulsive, negative, or circular "monkey mind" thought patterns, that's not helpful. But there's a way to go through the ruminating we often experience.

Years ago, I attended a seminar by intuitive guide Karen Hager and psychologist and astrologer Michael Lennox about developing a spiritual practice for personal growth.

One very helpful tool they talked about was consciously pointing your feelings in the direction you want to go. If your mind gets caught in a negative loop... stop. Then turn direction and proceed in a more beneficial direction.

Think of it as "Stop, pivot, and point."

Stop: If your mind gets caught in a negative, unproductive thought, or loop.

Pivot: Head in the other direction. Change your stream of thought.

Point: If that thought feels good or positive, point in that direction and keep going.

This is a basic principle behind the Law of Attraction,[3] a basic philosophy suggesting energy and resources follow the direction of our thoughts and intentions. Or simply put, positive thoughts bring positive results, while negative thoughts bring negative results.

You can't get a positive outcome from a negative mindset.

According to the Law of Attraction, every thought vibrates and radiates a signal, and every thought attracts a matching signal. Keep reaching for the feeling of relief. That becomes your point of attraction.

It's not always easy to stop a runaway, spinning mind. But it's a habit you can build on. If you catch yourself in a negative spiral, say to yourself, "Cancel, cancel, cancel." Then point in the other direction.

This is a simple principle to apply once you become more aware of the power of your thoughts and how they affect your mood and your life.

SOUND BATHS

Sound healing is the ancient practice of using sound and frequency to promote healing and deep relaxation. It's a form of passive therapy utilizing the soothing, vibrational soundscape of gongs, Tibetan singing bowls, echoes of nature, and binaural beats (subtle sounds or acoustic beats that affect your brain waves).

This gentle process helps soothe the nervous system and can help with stress management, anxiety, and sleep while improving focus and concentration.

It promotes calm, releases stress, and helps relax the whole body, slowing your breathing and soothing your emotions.

I've gone to several immersive sound baths in person and found these to be an incredibly lulling, full-body experience. Sound bath videos on YouTube are also available and effective—whether relaxing while lying down with headphones on or when soaking in a warm bath surrounded by candles.

However you experience it, sound healing is a powerfully satisfying experience.

MUSIC

It's important to be aware of how significantly music can affect your mood and evoke strong emotional responses, sometimes lifting you up with a sense of joy and calm—or lowering your mood deeper into despair.

Music can reinforce and validate your current emotional state and influence your emotional destination in either direction. To use a positive example, listening to upbeat music can motivate you to move your body or complete tasks.

Music can also evoke memories, happy or sad. Melancholic music has a place for a while; it can help purge deep emotions and release tears but try not to dwell there. It may seem obvious, but playing sad songs repeatedly while depressed can keep you stuck there.

Soft tunes—spa music, classical, piano, or nature sounds—can be a small first step in positively influencing your mood and behavior.

Research has shown that music can also have a positive impact on your health by reducing heart rate and blood pressure, lowering stress hormones, and boosting the happy ones.

"A music playlist that gradually moves from uncomfortable emotions to comfortable ones can be a healthy coping strategy and facilitate a positive mood change,"[4] according to musical therapy professionals.

TAKE A VACATION FROM GRIEF

Because grief has the potential to be all-consuming, and, therefore, draining, it's important to give yourself a reprieve from time to time for your well-being.

A vacation from grief can be a much-needed time-out from a busy mind and stressed body—whether it's just a 15-minute breather, a full weekend, or longer.

Keep it light and easy. Go see a movie, attend a concert, or watch a play. Enjoy a spectator sport, stroll through an art gallery or zoo, visit the park; have a picnic, and put your feet in the sand or grass, get a massage, treat yourself to a manicure or pedicure, read a good book or have someone read to you, or just wander and discover a new place.

Get out of the house. Leave grief at home.

What did you like to do as a kid? Try that. And treat yourself to an ice cream cone.

CREATIVITY

Developing a regular creative practice can be an effective healing outlet and way to express your loss. Activities can range from creative writing to coloring, cooking, painting, scrapbooking, vision board making, gardening, photography, or whatever inspires your imagination.

What did you love doing when you were young? Remember the whimsy that was your life back then? Allow yourself to revive some of that playful, creative spirit.

Tapping into your imaginative side can be a meditative process in itself, providing a distraction from grief and allowing you to focus on something positive and constructive.

Creativity takes your mind out of grief and closer to the natural joy inside.

COMFORT TV

Experts say watching your old favorite television shows or movies can have positive psychological benefits.[5] They can bring you back to a simpler time when there were fewer responsibilities or worries.

When I'm sad or depressed, I can binge on shows like *Friends*, or the series I grew up with when I need some "comfort TV." I seem to never tire of them.

Our familiar old shows seem to trigger happy, stress-free memories and are like the favorite foods we grew up with.

I just didn't know why. Experts say it's because television from the past gives us a sense of safety and security in a chaotic world. We know what to expect and simple consistency—when things otherwise feel out of control—can be calming.

Some people may also remember bonding with their parents, watching shows together as adults or as children. Putting these programs on again can bring back that "connected" feeling.

Our favorite shows or movies can be useful tools in dealing with mild anxiety and depression. So, tune in to those familiar memories; there's a reason it feels good.

LAUGHTER

There is a healing power to laughter.

According to studies, a key inner resource for coping with life (and death) is humor. It acts as a buffer between us and the negative effects of stress while making a tough situation a little bit more bearable.[6]

Together with psychological benefits, the Mayo Clinic shows many positive short and long-term benefits of laughter, including stimulating the heart, lungs, and muscles. Increasing endorphins relieves stress and lessens depression and anxiety while lifting your mood.

It can also be a surprising respite from grief.

When I need a mental break, funny movies, sitcom bloopers, funny animal compilations on YouTube, or silly reels on various social media sites can take me out of my head and lighten my energy.

I also like reminiscing about funny moments with my parents that still make me laugh. I feel close again to them when I do, and it always seems to be an effective way to release sadness.

It feels good to laugh, even if sometimes it's through tears.

Touchstones

As an easy way to stay grounded and focused on the positive aspects of life, I keep special touchstones around my house. These are gentle reminders that subtly reach below the conscious mind and reinforce positive feelings.

They really do help!

My favorites are words of encouragement written on rocks or shells, with simple messages like "Know Peace," "Love," "Choose Happiness," and "Courage." If you can't find these in your local store, simply pick up a smooth rock and, with a marker, write your own message.

A touchstone can also be any object that represents your loved one or a special memory. It's another way to keep your connection and their memory close.

Find something that touches your heart and *feel in* its encouragement and comfort.

MEMORY AIDS

Temporary memory issues—and grief-related "brain fog"—are among the most common side effects of bereavement. There's no shame in relying on a few memory crutches for what can temporarily feel like a broken brain.

I can't tell you how many times I went to the grocery store with a few simple items in my head but forgot them by the time I got there or burned something on the stove because a small distraction diverted my focus.

Grief brain can make the simplest things seem difficult.

When there are so many things swirling in your mind, it's easy to lose your train of thought, forget something you just committed to memory, get easily confused, and generally lose the ability to focus.

To help simplify things, *write things down*. Make "to-do" lists and prioritize tasks. Tape Post-it notes where you can easily see them. Use a timer or alarm clock if you're following a time-sensitive task.

Get these things out of your busy head and down onto paper.

Free your mind until it starts functioning normally again.

Color-coded sticky notes can also help. For example: Use green-colored notes for simple health reminders (take your vitamins, breathe deeply, exercise), orange for practical tasks (pay bills, errands, the shopping list, calls to make), etc.

I use yellow sticky notes to jot down simple, encouraging quotes or inspiring affirmations when needed.

Such assistance can lighten your mental load, organize your daily life, and be your personal cheerleaders.

THE POWER OF PETS

We don't need researchers to tell us (although they do) that our bonds with pets can help ease the grieving process.[7]

Stroking a dog or cat, for instance, increases serotonin and dopamine levels in the brain, lowering the stress, anxiety, and depression associated with grief. Whether they're furry, hairless, scaled, or feathered, creatures can provide affection and comfort during difficult and stressful times. Their presence can offer quiet companionship, reduce feelings of isolation, and provide a healing sense of routine and normalcy.

People often tell me they feel freer to grieve and cry in front of their pets than humans. There's no judgment, no reason to feel self-conscious in the company of animal companions. There's just love.

Pets of all kinds can be a comforting presence when no words can help, especially during those times when there's little energy for human interaction. Even the vibration of a cat's purr has been shown to have a healing effect. The low frequency of a feline's purring, typically between 25 and 150 Hz, is not only for communication but may have a therapeutic effect, according to scientific studies.[8]

Interactions with purring cats have been observed to reduce stress and anxiety in humans. This can lead to a decrease in cortisol (stress) levels and contribute to lowering blood pressure.

If you are an animal lover but don't have a pet of your own and can't adopt one, try spending time with a friend's or pet a passing puppy. All those scenarios can give you a happy boost.

Simplify Tasks

Because a grieving mind is difficult to focus, planning, organizing, and completing tasks can seem like monumental challenges.

Big projects can feel so overwhelming that they leave you feeling frozen or unable to know where to begin.

If this happens, try keeping your tasks simple. Break down tasks in ways that feel doable for you that day. Instead of cleaning the entire house all at once, make a list and go room by room over a few days.

If that's too big, break it down into smaller tasks like dusting one day, sweeping the next.

Simplifying tasks can help calm your nervous system and make things more manageable.

Body

> *"There is a time for everything, and a season for every activity under the heavens: a time to be born and a time to die, a time to plant and a time to uproot, a time to tear down and a time to build, a time to weep and a time to laugh, a time to mourn and a time to dance."*
>
> — Ecclesiastes 3:1-4

SLEEP

One of the common complaints among those grieving is how difficult it can be to get a good night's sleep. According to the Centers for Disease Control and Prevention,[9] seven or more hours per night is recommended on average for adults.

Although the hours of sleep you get are important, the quality of sleep is essential.

Here are some tips that help improve your overall sleep:

- Prepare the bedroom by making sure it's clean, decluttered, at a comfortable temperature, and dark
- Turn off electronic devices at least an hour before bed
- Stick to a regular bedtime and wake-up routine
- Ideally, avoid alcohol altogether and do not have caffeinated beverages after 3 p.m.
- Practice relaxation exercises before bed, such as breathing exercises, prayer, or meditation
- Listen to sleep hypnosis or guided meditation recordings
- Play soft music or soothing nature sounds. The sound of rolling ocean waves can be especially calming

Other suggestions that many I spoke with found useful include:

- A weighted blanket

These are therapeutic blankets that weigh between 5 and 30 pounds. The pressure from the extra weight mimics a therapeutic technique called "deep pressure therapy" to help calm the nervous system. It can feel like a safe hug. It's been said to help reduce anxiety, relieve symptoms of depression, and improve sleep quality.

- Aromatherapy & essential oils

Lavender is a popular aromatherapy oil believed to help with sleep. Candles, sleep mist for your sheets, lotion, and even lavender tea have been reported to help you relax before bed and usher in a better night's sleep. If you're not fond of the floral scent of lavender, try eucalyptus and spearmint. It's very refreshing and soothing.

- Bath before bed

A warm lavender Epsom salt bath—or one with 100 percent pure magnesium flakes—can soothe the mind, relax the body, and promote a better night's sleep.

- Natural remedies and supplements

CBD drops, melatonin, chamomile tea, ashwagandha, and kava have been reported as alternative aids for those who have trouble sleeping. (Keep in mind that supplements are not approved by the Food and Drug Administration. It's important to talk with a healthcare provider before starting any new supplement.)

POWER NAP

When your body is exhausted in times of grief, it's time for a temporary halt, regardless of what the world may be telling you.

What your tired body needs more than anything is a restorative break so it can rebuild.

If that means crashing on the couch for a few hours, do it.

A 10-minute power nap? Take it.

If you're feeling completely overwhelmed, it's okay to go back to bed for the day. Listen to your body. If you need to stay burrowed under the covers, allow yourself that.

These days won't last forever. For now, rest.

EFT TAPPING FOR GRIEF

Emotional Freedom Techniques (EFT or "Tapping") is a form of psychological acupressure based on the same meridians used in traditional acupuncture (but without needles). It combines traditional Chinese medicine with modern psychological acupressure techniques.

This holistic healing method is used to open energy pathways in the body and has been scientifically proven to help people who are experiencing grief. It can also help lower stress and anxiety and help with past trauma.

The process is simple; you can follow the practitioner or instructor. First, you'll think about a specific problem. Then, you'll be guided to tap with your fingertips along specific meridians on the head and body to stimulate kinetic energy while repeating positive affirmations intended to clear the emotional blocks.

There are many EFT specialists that can be found in private practice, or you can also access video demonstrations on YouTube that are specifically focused on grief healing.

These videos are short and effective, demonstrating how this painless technique can be an avenue to honor and slowly release any grief, pain, and tears that may arise.

DEEP BREATHING

It may seem silly to have to remind yourself to do something as simple as breathing, but when stressed or in grief, our breath tends to be shallow and muscles tense.

According to medical professionals, deep belly breathing can boost your energy, reduce stress, release anxiety, and alleviate depression. The practice is as follows:

1. Breathe in slowly and deeply through your nose, pushing your stomach out so that your diaphragm is put to maximal use.
2. Hold your breath briefly.
3. Exhale slowly through your mouth as you think of a peaceful word to yourself, such as "relax."
4. Repeat the entire sequence five to 10 times, concentrating on breathing deeply and slowly.

Deep breathing is straightforward yet powerful. You can do it at any time you feel tension or stress building. If you catch yourself feeling tight, even a few deep breaths can help.

The oxygen sent to your brain and nervous system will thank you, and you may just find your heart rate, anxiety level, and body tension going down.

Breathwork

Breathwork is a growing trend but has been around for thousands of years and has roots in yoga. It refers to breathing exercises that are intended to promote mental, physical, and emotional health.

More involved than just deep breathing, breathwork uses intentional, controlled breathing exercises to release toxins and stress when you breathe out and nourish your mind and body when you breathe in.

It's a mindfulness tool that can be an effective aid for centering into the present moment and helping to calm your nervous system.

Many experiencing grief enjoy this practice as a form of self-reflection, energy release, and getting out of their heads. For many, it's a fast form of relief.

Classes can be taken individually or in groups and are available in person, online, or with the help of YouTube videos.

Hydrate

When you're barely eating or resting, remembering to drink enough water and stay hydrated may be low on your priority list. But it's important.

After all, the human body is made up of roughly 60 percent water and needs it to function properly. Every cell, tissue, and organ in your body—especially your brain, which is approximately 75 percent water—needs it to deliver nutrients and remove toxins.

According to medical experts, when the body doesn't get enough water, brain cells become less efficient. Symptoms of even mild dehydration can include memory loss, poor focus, shortened attention span, and dizziness. Other grief symptoms like fatigue, headaches, and confusion, meanwhile, can worsen.

Have you ever experienced a lack of tears when crying? Doctors say it can be a sign of dehydration.

A good rule of thumb, they suggest, is to drink between half an ounce to an ounce of water for each pound you weigh each day.

For example, it is recommended that a 130-pound person drink at least 65 ounces a day.

Other drinks that can contribute to your daily water intake can include herbal teas, low fat milks, and milk alternatives, fruit and herb infused water, fruit juice, sugar-free sports drinks, and coconut water.

Adding sugar-free electrolyte powder to water is another good option.

If you are unsure if you are well-hydrated, there are simple ways to check. Common signs are dry skin, lips, and decreased skin elasticity, which you can test by lightly pinching the skin on the lower arm between two fingers and then releasing after a few seconds. (Hydrated skin will rapidly return to its normal position, while dehydrated skin will remain in a "tented" position and take much longer to bounce back.)

One trick I found helpful to drink more water: Get a carafe with lemon, cucumber, and/or mint with nice glassware, which makes hydrating a treat, not a chore.

Exercise

Moving your body is important for your health, healing, and emotional health.

It's understandable that when you're grief-stricken, your motivation isn't going to be high. But a strenuous regimen isn't necessary. Even a 10-minute walk around the block is a good start.

Physical activity can get your blood pumping, release endorphins, help manage depression, and improve your mood. It's also a healthy distraction from grief and a great form of self-care. It will literally start moving you forward and give you some momentum.

Easy exercises like stretching, yoga, tai chi for beginners, walking, light jogs, or riding an exercise bike can be good starting options. With more motivation or energy, try getting to the gym, running, or kickboxing (especially if anger is an emotion you are struggling with.)

The more often you exercise, the easier it will become and the better you will feel.

If you've been isolated, exercise can also help get you out of the house and back to the land of the living. Remember, emotions have their own energy, and you don't want to keep the low ones trapped in your body.

Somatic Work

It's often reported that the body and mind can feel disconnected while in heavy grief.

While traditional therapy works on thoughts and emotions verbally, somatic therapy has people tune into their physical sensations and emotions in order to process trauma, grief, and other difficult experiences.

The belief is our bodies store memories of everything that has happened to us, just like our brains do. Somatic therapy, which has been gaining popularity in recent years, works with several techniques like movement, mindful breathing, and body scans to release the imprint of stored trauma from a person's system.

It is believed unresolved grief, for example, can lodge in the body, leading to fatigue, tightness in the chest, sleep disturbances, anxiety, depression, and more, until it is processed and released.

I know many in grief who have found this form of therapy, with the help of a licensed somatic therapist, a refreshing addition to their recovery tool kit.

Pamper Yourself

When your body and mind need a little relief, pamper yourself. It's not self-indulgent; it's self-care. A little bliss can go a long way in resetting your nervous system.

Enjoy a massage—either at a day spa or through a licensed at-home massage service. Treat yourself to a facial. Get a manicure or pedicure. Enjoy a bubble bath with soft music and imagine the sadness washing away.

Buy yourself a bouquet of flowers. Or go on a relaxing stroll and pick your own.

Buy yourself a present and wrap it in a nice gift bag like you might do if you were thoughtfully giving it to someone else.

Cook yourself something nutritious and tasty. Or order a special dinner for delivery, especially dessert, and set the table like you would for a special guest.

And that guest is you.

Relax on the sofa with a cozy blanket, soft socks, and a good book or movie. Treat yourself to nice-smelling candles or build a warm fire.

Make time for you. Spoil and treat yourself in healthy ways.

That's what self-care is all about.

Soul

"One of the marvels of the world is the sight of a soul sitting in prison with the key in its hand!"
— Rumi

Remember: you are not your grief. Some say we are all spirits having a human experience.

But this human experience can weigh on our soul sometimes.

To help regain some inner balance and reconnect to yourself, consider experimenting with the following ideas and activities.

The Pursuit of Joy

Will I ever feel joy again? Sound familiar? There were times I felt so stuck in sadness that I couldn't even remember what it felt like to feel happy, much less how to find it again.

Tip: Write down what brought you joy *before* all this. Remembering the past is sometimes easier than imagining the future.

What did I enjoy before? I wrote activities down like a menu so I could slowly work them back into my life—walking by the ocean, finding new hiking trails, riding along the beach bike path with friends, attending art shows... Suddenly, I realized there *were* enjoyable things that I could look forward to.

I would have to start slowly, but having something to look forward to is *forward-thinking*. And that's the direction I needed to head.

Note: Experiencing joy while grieving is nothing to feel guilty about. That's a common reaction I hear repeatedly among the heavy-hearted in grief. It's normal and healthy to love yourself enough to allow a little bit of life back in.

When you're ready, a baby step forward is a giant leap toward your healing.

Meditation

Meditation is a technique designed to train the mind to focus while limiting irrational, negative, or repetitive mind chatter. It is important for life balance.

Meditation can be both a spiritual and therapeutic practice and can have long-lasting benefits for your mental health and quality of life. It can help you access a deeper state of self-awareness, improve your mood, promote better sleep, and foster mental resilience to help you cope with life's challenges.

You can meditate alone, follow YouTube meditations, or engage in a group with others. It can be lengthy or as short as a few minutes or so until you get the hang of it.

One of the most important things to remember is to do it any way that is best for you: sitting, standing/walking, or lying down.

Other benefits of meditating include releasing tension, getting into the present moment— instead of wallowing in the past or worrying about the future—and calming anxiety.

To start, Mindful.org offers these suggestions:[10]

1. Find a comfortable, quiet place to sit.
2. Set a time limit. 5-10 minutes to start is adequate.
3. Get your body comfortable. You can sit in a chair with your feet on the floor, sit on the floor, kneel, or lie down.
4. Focus on your breath. Follow as you breathe in and out. Feel this.
5. Quiet your mind. Go beneath the chatter. Notice when your mind wanders and just come back to your breath.
6. Close with kindness. Open your eyes if you have chosen to close them. Notice the sensation in your body and your surroundings. Observe your thoughts and emotions.

When meditation on your own is just too difficult, try guided meditations.

YouTube is a great resource for finding topics that may work for you. There are many to help with grief, inner peace, self-love, anger, anxiety, and even Yoga Nidra for insomnia.

If you find traditional meditation difficult, try a "walking meditation." As you walk, use all your senses. Look at the different colors all around. Listen to the wind and birds chirping or sounds of the city. Really listen. Feel the warmth of the sun. Breathe in and exhale with appreciation for this life.

This can take you more fully into the present moment, where there's no ruminating about the past or fretting about the future. This is what the calming power of "presence" is all about.

Meditation is helpful in grief because it allows you to focus and can help break the cycle of negative thinking that fuels depression and anxiety. It also allows you to sit with your feelings, which can lead to a cathartic release of emotions that ultimately calm the body and mind.

Don't be surprised if tears come; let them flow.

The goal of meditation is to quiet your mind and create a more serene inner world.

Prayer

Regardless of belief, prayer serves as a means for individuals to connect with their higher power and find guidance, strength, and solace. For many who grew up with a strong religious or spiritual foundation, faith can provide incredible comfort and direction during loss.

Fellowship at your place of worship can also bridge the separateness that so many feel while in mourning.

It can also prove to be a person's steadfast companion. Leaning into your beliefs can provide a soothing sense of power when you might otherwise feel utterly powerless.

Prayer not only benefits the spirit, but research has shown that prayer can have positive effects on mental and physical health, such as reducing stress and anxiety and improving overall well-being.

There is power in prayer; let it feed your hungry soul.

GROUNDING

If you've been grieving, you probably feel like your battery is drained. But you'll be happy to know there's a recharging station just below your feet.

This planet is like a giant battery that provides a natural charge from its core. If you've been feeling oddly outside your body, too much into your headspace, or like you need to recharge, a simple grounding exercise can often help.

"Grounding" is a centering practice that allows you to receive this nourishing energy from the earth. It allows you to be more fully in your body in the present moment.

It helps balance your physical and spiritual bodies, with results that boost your mood, reduce anxiety, pain, and inflammation, improve sleep quality, and help support brain function.[11]

To ground, do this:

1. Go barefoot.
2. Put your feet in the grass, in the sand, or on the earth. Wiggle your toes.
3. Imagine roots going from the soles of your feet down deep into the core of the earth. Imagine the earth's energy coming back up into you.
4. Breathe deeply.

Be fully in your body. Clear your mind and be completely in the moment. Learn to be still.

Some say you can practice grounding, also known as earthing, for as little as five minutes a day and notice a difference. Thirty minutes or more? Even better.

Let the natural energy of Mother Earth stabilize and fuel you.

BE IN NATURE

Like so many others, I find connecting to Mother Nature to be among the most peaceful and rejuvenating things I can do for myself. Nature is quiet but strong and replenishes the soul.

Being in nature helps keep you present as you tune out the busy world and take in your surroundings. She helps you anchor yourself in the moment by engaging all the senses.

There's also a proven healing power there.

Negative ions, generated by the movement of air and water, are everywhere in nature and can have several benefits, including boosting serotonin levels in the brain.

If you've walked by the ocean, listened to a waterfall, wandered through a forest, sat by a bubbling stream, or gone for a stroll after a rainstorm, you know what this feels like.

Negative ions have been studied for decades, and research has shown that they can help alleviate symptoms of depression, anxiety, and stress, promote better sleep, and reduce other health problems.[12]

Have you ever hugged a tree while out in nature? I'm a tree hugger and swear by it. If you've never done it, give it a try. They

are strong and have energy. Wrap your arms around its trunk and feel its strength.
Hold the moment. Feel.
That's Mother Nature's unconditional love hugging back. Her healing and comforting properties are all around.

Self-Nurturing

Few things can feel better for the soul than when you take a holistic approach to your healing. This includes taking good care of all aspects of the life you are rebuilding.
Learn to love yourself. Parent and protect yourself. Be compassionate to yourself.
Nurturing is different from pampering. Nurturing is the process of fostering and encouraging your growth in ways that will support your recovery from pain.
Treat yourself like you would a dear friend or loved one. Be kind, considerate, and gentle; protect your boundaries, allow yourself to fail, and still be forgiving.
To nurture your own being is to honor the child that grieves inside.

Connection & Community

It's natural to want to isolate yourself when we are grieving. While you might also be sensitive to overstimulation right now and not in the mood to talk, doctors say too much isolation can lead to depression.

When alone starts to feel lonely, a little community helps. There are still ways to get human interaction without exhausting yourself.

Try joining activities that involve other people but don't require too much social energy, like strolling through an art gallery, exercise or yoga class, painting lessons, going to church, or attending a spiritual seminar.

You don't need to say a word to be in a community and feel the goodness of others.

A little connection can sometimes be a nice, easy way to transition back into the world.

PART II:
Bereavement Support Community Forum

"One of the most important things you can do on this earth is to let people know they are not alone."

— SHANNON L. ADLER

CHAPTER 1

Walking Each Other Home

"Embrace your grief. For there, your soul will grow."

— CARL JUNG

Me with my dad, 2017

The Wounded Healer

In Greek mythology, Chiron symbolizes the wounded healer. After being poisoned and experiencing enormous pain, he used his trauma to heal others.

The "wounded healer archetype" is a concept developed by Swiss psychiatrist Carl Jung. When working as therapists, Jung proposed wounded healers may bring deeper and intuitive empathy, insights, and patience to their clients' work, sharing their own experiences and stories of struggle, vulnerabilities, and loss.

I believe this to be true, based on my own experience with doctors who had—or had not—lived through the death of a parent.

The ones who had lost one or both parents were able to harness the power of their personal pain and display a deeper level of compassion, which was validating, comforting, and healing.

Jung's model applies to people who are medical professionals, as well as those who are not. In fact, it's our own hurt that provides many of us in grief with the ability to help others. The capacity to offer healing support rests in listening to other people's stories, bringing your own self-awareness, and an open heart to help.

Whether we realize it or not—after the loss of our parents—we all have the power to become a wounded healer. Or, as Ram Dass, the well-known spiritual teacher of the 1960s and 1970s, put it so simply, "We're all just walking each other home."

In life, on this path, we need to take care of one another.

The Comfort of Community

Most everyone has parents or parental figures who raised them and whom they will one day lose.

It's the kind of shared experience or club that no one wants to be a part of.

But those who've known the loss of their parents are among the very few who can truly understand what it does to a person.

Grief can leave a person feeling incredibly lonely and misunderstood. Not everyone has family or friends who can understand the gravity of this particular kind of loss or how and why it affects us the way it does.

Our pain is real. It must be expressed and witnessed for us to process it all.

In the beginning, especially, there is a need for solitude. If you're like most people in this situation, you may feel disconnected from yourself *and* the world around you.

But to heal, we can't always do it alone. We need human support.

If you are isolated in your grief and need guidance and a listening ear, it can be beneficial to join a support group dedicated specifically to parental loss. It helps to be part of a community that recognizes and relates to this pain based on first-hand experience.

Connecting with others in these groups provides a safe space for sharing stories, gathering guidance, and finding solace. Such support can help normalize feelings of grief, offer validation, and help you work through confusing emotions and fears without apprehensions about judgment.

Bereavement support groups also provide a level of validation and belonging that may be hard to find elsewhere. You are likely to hear anecdotes and suggestions that can help you move forward.

Bereavement & Grief Support Group Types

In a post-Covid world, it's clear there are more choices and types of grief support groups than ever. Depending on your availability and comfort level, you might prefer in-person or online support, or a combination of both.

Following are a few things to consider when deciding what works best for you:

In-Person Groups: These groups typically meet on a regular basis on a set day and time, usually once a week or once a month. If you need to get out of the house and be around others, this can be the first step to help alleviate feelings of loneliness.

In-person meetings tend to be more intimate, with a smaller number of participants in the group. They are often structured and run by a facilitator to make sure conversations stay on point, with everyone given the opportunity to share.

Different losses bring different challenges. Many in-person groups are open to people dealing with loss in general: a child, spouse, parent, sibling, pet, etc. That's why it's helpful and most effective to focus on groups specifically tailored to parental loss.

Bereavement support groups aren't for everyone. Some individuals may be more private about sharing with a group of strangers. In the acute stage of grief, emotions are raw, and it can be deeply uncomfortable to sit side-by-side with others in deep pain when you have your own feelings to wrestle with. If that's the case, online groups may be preferable.

Online Groups: Online grief support communities are plentiful and provide the most flexibility. Some are run by professionals via their own websites. Others are less formal and peer-support driven. Online groups are most often free and you're more likely to find groups tailored to your type of loss.

Online support can be found on most social media platforms, like Facebook. These are convenient and can be accessed 24 hours a day, 7 days a week. (After my mother's death, I founded *Healing After the Loss of Your Mother – Grief Support,* and after my father's death, formed *Healing After the Loss of Your Parents – Grief Support* for those seeking comfort, guidance, and community. Both can be found on Facebook.)

With online groups, it's easier to remain anonymous, participate if you're comfortable, or scroll posts for insight. People who are shy or not ready to share their feelings may find online support a helpful first step in getting outside support and feeling less alone.

With online groups, it's easy to: check in or out as needed, unfollow if you find the posts too depressing, negative, or unhelpful. If you have a specific question, it's also easier to just post and wait for feedback or type your question into the search bar and pull up related posts.

Grief makes it difficult for many to find the energy for the support they need, much less leave the house.

If you're not ready to get out of your pajamas or enter the real world, accessing online support groups can be a good first step. These are especially helpful when there are no grief support groups in your local area.

Finding the Right Group

Which group is right for you? The one that feels healing rather than a burden. Most facilitators who run in-person groups suggest giving the group at least three tries. Maybe you'll find out if it clicks or isn't for you.

Every group has its own personality. Just find one that matches yours and try to embrace the benefits of what a group experience can offer.

To find an in-person support group, you can contact nearby hospitals, hospice companies, funeral homes, churches, synagogues, and other places of worship. You might also find local Meetup support groups.

To locate a nearby group, go online and search by typing in "grief support" or "bereavement support groups" and your zip code. You can also type in your city and "Department of Mental Health" for local grief-related resources and materials.

There are also nationwide organizations that offer help as well as directories for free in-person, local grief support, including:

Hospice Foundation of America (www.HospiceFoundation.org)

American Hospice Foundation (www.AmericanHospice.org)
GriefShare (a biblical, Christ-based grief support ministry at www.GriefShare.org)
Grief.com (www.Grief.com)

Unexpected Benefit

Whether online or in-person, it's a liberating feeling when you are given permission to speak freely, without judgment. There's also something magical that happens when you do: it helps you process faster.

A safe space is a healing space.

This sense of belonging can offer a safe harbor at a time when the world feels lonely and unpredictable.

Varied life experiences exist within these groups, which is a wonderful bonus. Not everyone had a rosy relationship with their parents. Maybe you have unresolved feelings that you hold inside because you're too self-conscious to share them with others. You don't want to feel judged or awkward about "speaking ill of the dead."

But sensations like guilt, resentment, jealousy, and anger are big ones to grapple with and understand on your own. We work through difficult emotions by venting and releasing.

When you find "your people" in a group that feels like home, you'll discover it's safe to share. Because every story has value, and it can be a healthy avenue for getting difficult feelings off your chest. This can help not only the person sharing but also others who might identify with it.

It's not just me" is a very reassuring realization.

By joining a group, you might gain valuable insights and understanding just by listening to others and tapping into different perspectives.

"Aha" moments may surprise you and come from unexpected places.

Most importantly, you'll learn where people believe they've made mistakes and yet made their way through this. Sometimes, all you need to keep going is a little direction or a drop of hope.

The surprising benefit of a group experience—I'm told time and time again—is how rewarding it can feel to know someone's heavy heart is a little lighter thanks to something you said or an experience you shared.

Uplifting others can also lift you up.

Isn't that what it's all about? Walking each other home?

CHAPTER 2

Peer Community Q&As

*"No one is useless in this world who
lightens the burdens of another."*

— CHARLES DICKENS

SOME OF THE BEST GUIDANCE and encouragement I have received as I worked my way through loss came unexpectedly from total strangers in bereavement support groups. I found a level of empathy and understanding that was not only soothing but healing.

In the beginning, I had so many questions that only someone who has lost both parents could answer. Many times, I was just looking for assurance that what I was feeling was "normal."

I also wanted guidance on how not just to survive but on how to thrive again.

How do you find joy again, I thought, when life feels so empty? How did they do it? How do I do it now?

When you see strangers helping people they don't even know—just because they understand your pain—that's when you see what "community" is all about.

When I turned to other adult orphans, I felt embraced in kindness. I didn't feel so alone. You don't have to, either.

The following two chapters are dedicated to common questions many in grief have posed, with answers from peers who share from their experiences and hearts.

I hope it provides not only guidance but also some of the reassurance and encouragement you may be searching for right now.

(For privacy, names associated with the following comments have been omitted.)

Losing Both Parents

Q: Did the death of your second parent feel different from the first loss?

"Yes, it immediately felt so very different. I just felt so alone."

"I was numb for weeks. I mean, I knew this day would one day come but losing them both left a different kind of hole in my heart."

"It's unbelievable how much the second-parent loss is stunning in its heartbreak and devastating to our sense of identity. I reverted to feeling like a child. And it makes you grieve them both simultaneously, ready or not, when you lose your second parent. The weight of losing both parents hit harder than I was prepared for."

"Losing my second parent reopened the grief of losing my first, which was hard enough on its own. My life had 'gone on' in time, but I was still working through a bag of issues after many years. I recently began therapy, which included talking about my grief, something I thought I had come to terms with. I hadn't and wish I had addressed everything sooner. Grief over one death, then the other was still there, beneath the surface, affecting other areas of my life. I'm glad I finally took the time to address it. I didn't realize how much not talking about my grief earlier impacted me in more ways than I could imagine."

"I feel like grief is compounded when we lose both parents."

"Losing both your parents is a big deal. It feels, sometimes, that only other 'adult orphans' understand the gravity."

"I felt alone. So incredibly alone."

"First, I felt shocked. Then numb. I thought, 'Here we go again,' but this was different. I could get through the grief, I had done it before, but I wondered how do I get through never having my mother and father in my life anymore? I just felt so empty."

"I'm a grown adult, but I feel like an orphan inside now."

"Untethered is how I felt and sometimes still feel. When you have one parent alive, there is some semblance of normal. When mine both died, life felt much different, like a part of me was gone forever."

"I lost my mom first and my world went upside down. It took years to return to whatever the 'new normal' is. My dad passed last June. I've cried and had my days, but I promised myself that I wouldn't lose myself again. I now know what to expect. I'm not going to lie, it is hard! Give yourself one day at a time. The natural flow of grief has a way of moving you through this again."

"I lost both my parents in a car accident 50 years ago when I was 15. I was their only son and child. That trauma, at that age, was a lot to work through. Therapy helped a great deal with the lost world I suddenly found myself in. No matter your age, we are not supposed to just get over grief and love... we are supposed to work through it. In our own time. One way we work through it is by finding others in the same situation who can show true empathy and support."

"I lost both my parents within months of each other, and my only sibling died when I was a child. It's sad to be the only one left. I'm only 38. I never imagined I would be alone so young, and despite having my own family, that's how I still feel. Alone. I'm so thankful for my kids and my husband, but I also live with the constant worry that I'll lose someone else."

"It felt like my foundation fell out from under me. It was a strange feeling. The positive change is I don't have the energy or interest to fight or be bothered by anything now. I felt empty and wasn't going to fill myself back up with anything toxic."

"I lost both my parents before I turned 29. While both losses were painful since I was close to them, nothing compares to the lonely, abandoned feeling that I was an orphan now. I have a loving husband and his family has sort of adopted me as their own, but it's still an empty feeling that my 'family' is conditional on my marriage."

"I'm in my 40s, and it surprised me how easily I reverted to feeling like a lost little child. Initially, there was a sense of reaching for security, and with neither parent there, I felt sheer panic. Thank goodness, that feeling didn't linger for too long."

"At first, I felt like a stranger in a strange land. It was the loneliest feeling. A year later, I feel like I've awakened to a new world with a new start. No expectations, and that doesn't scare me like it did in the beginning."

Tips & Advice

Q: What are some useful tips or advice for someone in the early days of grief?

"Be gentle with yourself. We must remind ourselves that losing a lifelong family member is a serious life event. There are smoother days ahead as we move through grief. I promise you that."

"Talking to friends who have lost both parents has helped me more than anything. They just get it. The bonus is these relationships are more real now. As a result, I value them more than ever before."

"Losing both parents changes you. It just does. Life became more manageable when I just accepted this basic truth after months and months of denying it."

"The initial aftermath is so hard. Nothing will really help but time and patience as you feel your way through. Cry a lot. Don't block your feelings; they'll just fester, and you'll have to deal with them later. It's called a 'process' for a reason. Just take it slow."

"Find a safe place where your grief will be honored and you will feel supported: friends, counseling, support groups. Loneliness is the hardest part. Let kind people help you."

"Reading books about connection to spirit or life after death gave me encouragement and hope that I will be reunited with my parents one day."

"If you pursue counseling, be sure to find someone who specializes in grief and bereavement. You'll get more out of it that way."

"I cried and cried. There isn't much you can do in the early days after a death, but this basic human release is so important."

"I found GriefShare to be a real lifesaver. For me, it was like other bereavement support groups but with a biblical viewpoint, which I liked. The weekly videos, workbook, and practical advice from the counselors and pastors are very helpful."

"Grief is not something we can just 'get over.' Getting through it takes time and honest self-reflection. If you've done it once, you have the strength to do it again."

"If you need even a little support or answers, try your nearest hospice agency. They are required to provide free grief counseling to community members and their counselors are trained in bereavement."

"Losing both parents was a different kind of grief. I found a wonderful grief counselor to help me through the early days. Things really changed when I started somatic exercises. The physical pain from stress and trauma was excruciating and trapped in my mind and body until I rehabilitated my nervous system with these exercises. I wish I had known about it sooner."

"I belong to multiple grief support groups. After my mother's death in 2013, they were a lifeline and helped me through a period I never thought I would survive. When my father died two years later, I was devastated, but the pain was not as penetrating. Being around others in those groups was a comfort. Over time, participating in these groups became less about my own loss and more about trying to encourage others, which feels healing."

"Not everyone had a good relationship with their parents. I didn't talk about their death for a time because I felt guilty that I wasn't grieving; instead, I felt relieved. When I listened to others talk about similar rocky parental experiences, I felt an incredible weight lift. I felt freer to live life for me now."

"You're going to deal with many different emotions as you mourn; just take it one day at a time. Do what's best for you. My mum has been gone for 45 years and my pappa for 9 years and I still miss them every day. This is normal. It helps to share stories and memories of them. It's even better if someone shares memories of them with you."

"People can be quick to dismiss any of those tortuous feelings of guilt, regret, or the 'what ifs' and 'whys' thinking they're helping relieve your pain. But I can tell you, the weight of holding this all in is heavy and real. These thoughts are freed by verbalizing your honest pain. My therapist told me that even if there's no answer, these questions deserve to be asked. Find someone who will listen. Get it off your chest. That helped me a lot."

"I became unable to relate to my friends after my parents died in my early twenties. No one else had experienced that magnitude of loss. That just made my feeling of isolation worse. Connecting with other adult orphans helped normalize what I was going through and provided the compassion I desperately needed. To be seen and understood is so comforting."

"The release of sadness, anger, longing through crying is incredibly important. I don't show my emotions to others, so I cry mostly on car rides alone. I also scream in the middle of the woods. It feels great for me, but I'm not sure what the neighbors think."

"When my dad died in 2006, I really hit the bottle hard and lost myself for a while. I wanted relief from the pain, but all it did was make my depression and anger worse. I decided I couldn't do that again after my mom's recent passing. She'd be so disappointed in her boy. I heard a great quote in one group: 'Raising your glass in celebration is one thing, but we should never drink our grief.' Wise words. I realize now the importance of finding constructive ways to release the hurt, not bury it."

"Grief is hard enough, but it hurts even more if your family disintegrates. The lack of interest in healing our family rifts left me even more heartbroken and alone. I tried and tried and struggled for some kind of resolution until someone shared this advice, 'It's not your job to fix something you didn't break.' I had to let the expectation of 'family' go and that is a hard secondary loss for many of us."

"When I couldn't breathe, eat, sleep, or stop the flow of sobs, I took a jacket that smelled like my mom and laid in bed with it. Being able to smell her helped me feel a part of her was with me. I also keep a bottle of my dad's cologne because one sniff helps me on days I really miss him. Both are very soothing and make me feel still connected to them."

"Animals and mother nature can help you appreciate life. They are the best grief companions."

"The exhaustion definitely takes a toll in the beginning, physically, mentally, and emotionally. Try to remember this is a temporary stop. When I was in the first few months after loss, I told myself if I could allow my feelings and grief, I'd be able to get back to my life, friends, and the gym sooner. It helped, and everything was still there when I got stronger."

"I saw a Tyler Perry interview with Oprah, where he said how grief is a very living thing. He said it visits at random. You can't schedule it. Can't work or drink it away. All it does is wait for you to finish. So now when it shows up, however it shows up, he just lets it. I learned to surrender to the process. When tears show up, let yourself cry without apology."

"The adjustment it takes to live a life without your parents is challenging for all of us. You are not alone in this. It hurts the most early on but have faith that the pain will recede with time and when you fill your life with other meaningful relationships and experiences."

"This pain is temporary. Remind yourself of this every day, take deep breaths, and believe in your ability to survive. Look how others did it and know you can too."

REGAINING BALANCE

Q: What can help with forward movement when trying to regain some balance in your life?

"Adding some healthy structure and routine to my life, which was consumed by grief, helped establish some needed balance. Without small tasks to move me forward, I'd just dwell on my pain and spiral."

"Sometimes it feels overwhelming and impossible to get out of this pit of hopelessness. You're not alone! To get out of the cycle of funk, I'd do one small act of self-care each day. Do this in baby steps. Small steps forward begin... one step at a time."

"I went into counseling for a short time when I felt a little stuck. It was very healing to have a space where your grief is allowed to be present. I try not to let it out at work, so therapy is my safe space to say all the things and feel all the feelings. If you try it and don't click with your therapist, it's okay to try a different one. It has been very helpful for me."

"After my second parent died and my role as his caregiver was done, I was ready for some normalcy, and I vowed not to feel guilty about that. I knew my parents were strong, and now I would be too. The 'firsts' are so hard, but I gently let myself feel everything. Time does help. I told myself I had already endured the loss of my first parent, and I could do it again."

"I can get bogged down in a spiral of negativity. Acknowledging and feeling your feelings is healthy. Dwelling in the long-term is not. Lately, as soon as I notice that starting up, I will say to myself, 'Not today!' and it helps me become more aware and prevents me from sitting in a puddle of negativity. It's a different kind of self-care that keeps me moving forward."

"It's been just over two years for me and I am starting to feel like myself again. The little tasks, washing, cooking, showering were all overwhelming in the beginning. Look after yourself, practice self-love, and take small steps at a time. We do get through this phase."

"In the first weeks and months, I was counting down the hours so I could fall asleep and forget. It would then start again the next day. It's going to take time. Reading books on grief and listening to podcasts helped me somewhat, but time is really the only thing that will get you to the other side. It was three years last month, and I still think about my parents every day, but I feel more balanced in my life again."

"My parents both died almost twenty-two years ago, and back then, I thought I'd never make it through or have a life again. While some degree of grief never goes away, the fresh pain does. Taking it all slowly helped me survive it and have the happy life I have today. You will make it through this painful time."

"Get out of the house and sit outside in the sun for a little bit each day if you can. Stamina for chores, kids, family, and managing your grief is hard. In the beginning, I had to set 15-minute timers for chores. Once that timer goes off, go rest or continue if you choose. Be kind to yourself."

"It's taken me about a year to start feeling a little like myself again. What's pushing me now is setting short-term goals, even something as simple as reading a new book or getting back into an exercise routine helped move me forward."

"A loss this painful can sometimes send our body chemicals into overdrive and we need help to get them back in line. Be open to talk therapy in addition to medication to help align your body if you're feeling overwhelmed for too long. There's no shame in needing and asking for help! As my dear friend said to me, 'If you had a broken bone, you'd see a doctor. A broken heart sometimes needs a doctor too.'"

"There is a season to grieve, but when you are open to life again, I found nature is the original antidepressant! Trees don't judge you, birds don't interrupt, and fresh air doesn't come with side effects. Unplug, unwind, and let nature work its balancing magic."

"When I lost my parents, I also lost what was left of my family of origin. It felt incredibly lonely. To regain some balance, I joined a non-denominational church, then a few women's groups, which brought back a form of 'family' that I craved. We need other people. I have a tendency to isolate, but having a community to be a part of helped me transition back to reality better. If the church isn't your thing, finding people going through what you are going through, or who share similar interests, can make a huge difference in being able to move forward."

"I started going for long walks with a friend every morning, which helped me start my day off in a more positive way. I was so depressed initially that I barely recognized myself. Getting out of bed felt impossible. A year later, I'm building myself back up, slowly, day by day."

"My husband stepped up for me and was understanding and supportive. That was everything. I don't know how I would have gotten through my grief without him. If you don't have a partner, rest in the company of an understanding friend or even grief support group members. They can offer so much validation because they 'know.' We don't have to carry heavy loads alone. Lean into the support of others… we all need help through."

"Initially, everything feels out of balance. Simply allowing yourself to feel bad for a while is a start. Make your health a priority. Then slowly add things back into your daily routine; it has a way of balancing things out again."

"I often feel that other orphans are my people. Any time I have a common interest with others, there is always this part of me that strongly doesn't fit in. I've realized there's just no way anyone else can really 'get me' unless they've lost their parents. Regaining balance meant finding my tribe; they fit and define genuine companionship."

Juggling Grief with Closing an Estate

Q: How do you balance both the need to grieve with the obligations of closing an estate?

"This can all feel so overwhelming, I know. There's an old saying about 'how do you eat an elephant?' One bite at a time. I had it all on me, but I did not hurry myself. Designate maybe an hour or less each day to just make a step of progress in terms of the estate. Delegate what you can. Grief alone will make you feel overwhelmed. Self-care is important, but we tend to put it on the back burner when our to-do list is calling. Make appointments with your grief. Go into silence at night before bed and express yourself with tears, journaling, or art. This is hard stuff but not impossible. You will find your way."

"There are no time limits on deciding what you will discard, keep, or donate. Now isn't a great time to make snap decisions. I did and regretted it. Store everything if you have to until you are ready. Make this very difficult step as simple as you can."

"Handling the estate was the toughest part for me, even beyond the loss. I made some hasty, unwise decisions when managing my parents' estate. Take your time if you can and deal with it when you are ready. Manage it in small steps. Now a little over two years later I look back with some regret and realize I was not thinking clearly and just wanted it all to be over."

"Give it time. Unless you are financially in need, there isn't any need to rush things. It's nearly two years since my parents both died, and we are only just selling their house now. Also, get as much help and support as you can. You need someone who won't hurry you but will share the difficult decisions gently with you and respect your feelings."

"My last parent to pass lived in an apartment, so her belongings had to be out pretty quickly. I packed it all and put it in my garage until I was mentally ready to go through her stuff. It's been four years, and I still have one large plastic container I haven't opened."

"There's your personal grief, then there will be the grief of packing up years of memories when cleaning out a home, and the pressure of dealing with legal matters. It helps to acknowledge that there's a lot to deal with all at once. I made grief my priority, gave it my attention in the morning, and dealt with business-related issues in the afternoon. Deep breaths help, along with recognizing that it's no easy task to juggle all of it."

"It's heartbreaking to deal with the practical side of grief, like packing up and selling the family home. Though it's so emotionally draining, it's worth it in the end if you can take your time. Allow yourself to relive those good memories, to reminisce. I categorized and sub-categorized tasks to make them easier to tackle. Take it day by day. Take breaks and remember to spend time doing what you love in between those times."

"I had a relative help me, but I went through a ton of grief and heartbreak."

"I felt that I had to focus on getting the estate settled before I could really grieve and let it out. It was a lot of extra pressure and, if I'm honest, I had a lot of resentment that it was getting in the way of grieving properly. Juggling both is tough to deal with for any son or daughter. It just is. Give yourself that acknowledgment, take it slow if you can, and find someone you can vent to."

"I had to remind myself to take small steps, one step in front of the other. I also brought in the support of friends, and therapy helped me manage the full load. I did fall into depression and took antidepressants for several months, which helped as well. As a man, asking for help has always felt taboo, but I'd encourage everyone to learn to accept help. There is no shame in being human."

CAREGIVER BURNOUT

Q: Did you experience "caregiver burnout?" How did you recover?

"Caregiver burnout is real! I shut myself off for a long time, to be honest. I don't think it did me any harm either. I have a low threshold for certain types of people now and have narrowed my world down. I'm also becoming more aware of the downside of people-pleasing and giving at the expense of my own happiness. I'm benefitting from a new focus on self-care now."

"My therapist told me that when you lose a parent, your tolerance for drama and B.S. is at an all-time low. It's even more difficult when you've spent so much energy caring for ailing parents. People can be disappointing, and it especially stings when you're so vulnerable and raw. Now is the time to step back and focus on caring for yourself."

"You now need to heal and take care of yourself. Feeling burnt out after the exhaustion of caregiving is a normal and healthy reaction. You need to refuel your energy—mind, body, and spirit—because you're probably running on empty. I was running on adrenaline for so long that fatigue followed, and I had zero tolerance for other people's whining, insignificant problems, and pointless chit-chat. All that just makes you realize how wiped out you really are. We all need to take good care of ourselves, make ourselves a priority, rest, and acknowledge what we went through. It's imperative to take a break from helping others while you recharge."

"I'm glad I was able to take care of my parents in the end, but I had a bad case of caregiver burnout after their deaths. I gave so much energy and time for years, then had nothing left. I had no patience for anyone's drama or even simple requests. I had to learn to start giving myself the same degree of care that I had been directing outward all those years."

"I lost my parents 10 months apart and each loss was utterly exhausting. I rested and slept as much as I could, and the only exercise I could tolerate for about a year after were leisurely walks. I called supportive friends, spent time in nature, went to therapy, and minimized my interactions with toxic people and entertainment. Now is your time to rest and do what you need to do to nourish your body and soul."

"I gave my all for so long and finally felt the crash, like I don't have any more to give. I finally put myself first in order to heal."

"I was exhausted. Burned out. Nothing left to give anyone and resentful when someone did pull on me for anything. My doctor said I was showing all the signs of adrenal fatigue after the years of chronic stress that came with being a caregiver. He said the adrenal glands can become exhausted by the demands of the ongoing fight-or-flight state in the body that chronic stress causes. It takes a toll on the body over time and, boy, did I feel it. I had to tackle the root cause, which was stress, and focus on regaining healthy balance in my life."

"I experienced severe caregiver exhaustion but learned a valuable lesson that will help me for the rest of my life... I learned to say 'no' and make myself a priority now."

"It takes time to fill your empty cup. Focus on mind and body care. You need it and you deserve it."

"Caregiving for elderly parents is a 24/7 job, even if they're not living with you. I lost all patience for people pulling at me when I had no time for myself, and nothing left to give. In the past four years, I have had two kids, lost both parents, and felt absolutely depleted. It's a new world after your parents' die, and the new world includes taking care of yourself like you did for them."

"My nerves and energy were shot after being a caregiver for the last nine-plus years. I was just so tired. I'm starting to feel better after spending the last three months truly resting as much as possible and focusing on myself. It felt strange at first, but it's getting easier to do things just because I 'want' to do them, not because I should or have to. I realize now that I was living in fight or flight mode, constantly waiting for the next emergency to pop up, but I feel extra rest has helped give my nervous system the much-needed reprieve it required."

RETURNING TO WORK

Q: Any tips for returning to work while grieving?

"My therapist gave me some great guidance. She said 'compartmentalizing' grief is a coping mechanism that separates the heavy emotions associated with loss and temporarily sets them aside so that you can focus on other areas of life, like your job. That doesn't mean walling off grief, but rather creating boundaries to prevent grief from overwhelming every aspect of our lives. By compartmentalizing grief, we allow ourselves the space and time to heal while still functioning in our daily lives."

"I was thankful for the schedule. I kept up with what had to be done. The thing with grief is that the emotions come bursting through at unexpected times. And sometimes awkward times. The key for me was to let it flow because I learned it would pass almost as quickly as it came. Step away if you need to in the moment. There is no shame in grief. Allow space in each day to let the grief flow. Grief is a long process, so try your best to kindly keep your life going. And maybe, give yourself a break from being perfect."

"I was self-employed and worked from a home office. I was fortunate that I had space to rest, cry, and grieve in private. The only hard part of returning to a normal daily workload was staying focused and motivated. I started slowly, a few days a week at first, and kept a schedule to help maintain structure and self-accountability."

"I was working in an office environment after my last parent died. Depending on your coworkers, they may say nothing or express condolences. Once you get through that, they'll return to business as usual. Hang in there. It's tough but just take it one step at a time. And know you're not alone; so many of us have endured loss and made it through. You will too."

'I actually looked forward to returning to work. I needed some balance from the grief-focused world I was in at home, a vacuum that left me feeling disconnected from daily life."

"I went back to work exactly two weeks after my mom unexpectedly passed away. I was there physically doing my job but mentally somewhere else. It kept my mind a little distracted, which was a good thing while I braced myself for the grief I'd allow to come later. Most people were respectful and didn't dig for details, but others... not so much. Be prepared for both."

"I work in sales and couldn't hide from the public, even though I found it hard to function. If I found myself choking up in the beginning. I was pleasantly shocked to see how kind and compassionate people—even total strangers—can be. We've all been through some kind of loss or tragedy. It's possible to be professional and still be human."

"Make use of routines. Create more of them wherever you can. The more structure your job has, the better; it will help to have something regular and expected in your day. And do make time to take a break, even if it's just five minutes for fresh air or quiet. During those break times, focus on breathing and know that this acute stage of grief will not last."

"Be prepared that you may experience some performance issues until you regain some emotional balance. We have all been there. If you need to take a moment to step away, that is understandable. Remember that deep breaths are important to help regulate your nervous system."

"Returning to work is hard. For me, I had such brain fog, and it was hard to stay focused. But I will say getting back, being around people, and staying busy helped a great deal."

"Take a deep breath and plunge right in. If someone expresses condolences and you don't want a conversation, just nod, say 'thank you,' and move on."

"I am so fortunate that my new job has been remote, so when I feel those 'grief moments' coming on, I am at home. It has helped me navigate the ups and downs. I can sleep longer and work on my self-care in between. Be gentle on yourself as you get back into some semblance of a new life without your loved one. One day at a time, as they say."

"If you cry, just know you are not alone. I'm in healthcare, and it can be hard to take care of myself when my job is to take care of others. It was just too much. I was always embarrassed by these unexpected tears, but it tapered off in time. Those around me showed a lot of grace. I realized I needed to show myself the same."

How Have You Changed?

Q: How has losing your parents changed you?

"I have a deeper appreciation for the value of time. I don't waste it on toxic people, and I invest it where I find joy."

"Being an adult orphan has changed me 100 percent. I'm not the person I was before, and I am just finding my way through this. It's a new world when you start living for yourself and no longer worry about winning your parents' approval or disappointing them. I'm sad, very sad, but I feel a certain freedom I've never felt before."

"I first thought losing my parents would break me. Then I realized how strong I am, and after having gone through that, I know I can withstand anything life throws at me. I have more faith in myself now."

"I have such a deeper appreciation for the fragility of life. I take in the small moments now. I say 'I love you' more freely. I live more fully."

"I lost my mother nine years ago, and my father's been gone almost two years now. I'm doing better than I was, but darn, your parents will always be your parents. Your security. I have extended family and a child I am grateful for, but I have a constant fear of losing people now. On the positive side, I also love harder than I ever have."

"I lost not only both my parents but also the only family unit that I had. I felt incredibly isolated for a time, but good friends have since become my cherished, chosen family. Life is different, but I find simple solace in more things like my dogs and also nature."

"I had to accept the concept of change when I prefer a tidy, safe life. That includes losing the people we love. It's the most difficult lesson to learn, but once we accept that painful fact, adapting in this new world becomes a little easier. We have no other choice and I'm growing more content with the new normal I am creating."

"It is not an easy bridge to cross; I'm still working on it years later. A lot of things have changed within me, with my relationships with those around me. But nothing scares me anymore, not even the thought of my own death. I have started valuing time more. There is little time left and so much more to do, so I'm doing as much of my life as I can now!"

"On one hand, I felt overwhelmingly alone in a very childlike way and missed my parents deeply. But, and with some guilt, I also felt free to do whatever I wanted to do now. The exhausting caregiving years were over. I could move across the country or just follow my dreams without fear of abandoning or disappointing them. Their opinion always mattered. The only one that counts now is mine. I felt a bittersweet sense of freedom."

"I am 62 years old and thought I flew the nest when I left for college years ago. Despite having my own family, a wonderful home, and a husband, it wasn't until both my parents died that I really felt I had no nest to return home to. That was just a strange and lonely feeling. I guess the child inside us is the one who grieves most when both parents are gone."

"I try to honor my parents rather than grieve them. We never get enough time, even if they live a long life. I'm more reflective now and have had to grow up. Death can change you, but it can't change your love."

"I feel I have a different purpose for living now. At first, I felt like a part of me died when my parents did. Years later, I feel like a part of me is living life again in ways that show my love for them and their memory."

"I'm not the same person I was when my parents were alive, and not the same person I was just after their death. We adult orphans become a little different due to our experiences and what we gain from it all: We become compassionate, understanding, and caring. I believe most of us have deeper empathy for others as a result, which will come back to us a thousand times over."

CHAPTER 3

Healing Roundtable: Advice, Guidance & Hope

"Our human compassion binds us the one to the other—not in pity or patronizingly, but as human beings who have learned how to turn our common suffering into hope for the future."

— NELSON MANDELA

I HAVE LEARNED MUCH, FOUND unexpected fellowship through some early dark days, been inspired, and garnered valued guidance from various support groups through the years; first after the death of my mother and then after the death of my father.

Because losing both parents was very disorienting for me, I wanted to learn more from others, in further detail, about their personal stories and see how they rebuilt a life after such a loss.

I decided to bring together a group of individuals who have lived through this complicated life stage and who have some distance from it now: from three to 55 years since their last parent's death.

I knew their seasoned perspectives could shed more light, insight, direction, and hope for all of us walking behind them.

I wanted to see, in the longer term, how we do this grief and healing thing. How do we get our life back on track and create our "new normal"? How did they do it?

So, I gathered 12 people—ages 36 to 81—for an intimate "healing roundtable" conversation to share their stories about the adult orphan experience, talk about how it changed them, what helped and what didn't as they worked to recover from loss and made their way through.

The participants come from varied backgrounds, all with different life stories. Some had positive relationships with their parents, others had fractured or complicated ones.

The vulnerability and truth these individuals are willing to share lets us know that everyone's experience is different. What is clear, however, is that we all grieve when our parents die and it changes us.

While each situation is highly personal and unique, there is a commonality to double parental loss that emerges from each story, as you will see.

The group of open-hearted individuals includes:

- James, 67, Brooklyn, NY
- Shyrl, 72, Redondo Beach, CA
- Kimberly 59, Murrieta, CA
- Linda, 70, Studio City, CA
- Judy, 68, Burbank, CA
- Michael, 70, Los Angeles, CA
- Annette, 81, Austin, TX
- Eileen, 60, Eugene, OR
- Susan, 59, Santa Monica, CA

- Theresa, 68, Washington, D.C.
- J. J., 64, Rancho Mirage, CA
- Marly, 36, Sedona, AZ

1. How Was Losing Both Parents Different From When You Lost Your First Parent?

James: I think the thing people commonly feel—and the word that comes to mind most often—is "orphaned." I felt like an orphan. When you lose your mother, the ultimate umbilical cord is cut between universes and realities. When your father dies, it's more like the ground comes out from beneath you. You lose your foundation. When you lose both of them, you feel groundless and lost. A terrible kind of floating. Because now, and it's harder if you're younger, you have to ground yourself, and feeling attached isn't enough, even to your sibling or siblings if you have any.

Shyrl: My mother dying about 12 years before my father created a lot of stress for me because my father was completely dependent on her. She handled the money, bill paying, medical care, etc., as well as dealing with his larger-than-life personality and quirks. All my focus was on getting him through his terrible grief. I spent a week with him to handle the legal things and made sure that I connected with his many friends from his church to make sure they would be there for him since my folks had moved to Nevada 30 years previously.

Kimberly: Losing both parents was definitely different than losing my first parent. First of all, I think all children grow up with the fear of losing their parents at some point. My kids fear it every day, and I fear it too. We know it will happen, but nothing prepares you for that day when it does happen. I'm also an only child, so the fear was significant.

We lost my dad suddenly, so neither my mom nor I was prepared for that. We dealt with it because we had to. There was a lot of shock. My mom was extremely angry and depressed, and as the only child, I had to take care of her because her health was very poor, and she was not functioning well. I went into immediate caregiver mode.

My father's death was complicated by the fact that my marriage was breaking up at the time, and I had two small children. So, I moved in with my mom and took care of her. Even though it was hard on both of us, we had each other's security.

When I lost her three years later, it was, of course, even more devastating because my last safety net, my last emotional attachment to a parent, and my last great relationship with my mom was gone. I was, in fact, now an orphan because I was an only child, and both my parents were only children.

It was tough. I was a divorced woman with two small kids and no parents. All my friends were married and having no one other than friends to look out for me was hard. They're all busy with their own lives and families, and even though I got support from them, I felt very alone in a way I had never felt before.

Linda: I lost my mother in my twenties to cancer, which was an extremely traumatic time. I had lost a dear friend to gun violence the month before; my mother, who had planned my wedding from her hospital bed and came home for the day but was clearly in pain and went back the same night only to pass away a month later, her funeral falling on my birthday.

It took a long time to stop reeling from that and through the years. I became very close to my father. Starting a family and realizing all that was lost to my mother never eased. She was robbed, and time became so precious with my father. I was lucky to have him until he was almost 96 years old. I cared for him a lot in his last years—through dementia and many health issues. While my mom's passing was brutal and I got my dad for so long, losing him was and still is pretty tough.

Judy: Losing my first parent, my mother, was very different than losing them both. I lost my mom to cancer when she was 63, and I was just 40. As I look back, losing my first parent—especially because she was my mom—was very different than losing my dad. The first time doing anything comes with a lot of new feelings, and along with that, there was always concern about my family, my sisters, and my father. I didn't really let it sink in on a personal level because I was too busy juggling tasks amid this new sense of responsibility.

My mom was a very strong and determined woman. She was the matriarch. Super strong woman. Determined. Realistic, fatalistic. There wasn't a lot of coddling over her health in my family. There wasn't a lot of room for weakness or vulnerability in my family, which is probably why I handled her death the way I did. By the time she did pass after a six-year health battle, we had some time to adjust.

I think I was more grateful that she went peacefully in the end—instead of the trauma she would have gone through—than I worried about what it would be like not to have her here.

I lost my dad six years later, and the difference was I felt 'orphaned.' I'm sure that's a feeling many feel when you're suddenly no longer someone's child, and that's a *strange* feeling. My sisters and I would talk about it. We were suddenly the matriarchs of the family, which was a coming-of-age moment.

My family remained close. It felt surreal to realize that the same way I used to look to my parents for protection, love, and support, now I'm the one people will look to for these things. It made me realize I have to mature a little bit.

Michael: My father died 35 years ago when I was 35; my mother died three years ago when I was 67. I felt devastated when my first parent died, but my mother was the central figure in our nuclear family. She ruled the roost, so I felt the impact of her loss more deeply. When she died, I felt *unmoored*.

Annette: After 52 years, it's a little hard to reconstruct my exact feelings and emotions. But in my case, the loss of my first parent, my mom, was extremely difficult as we were very close. However, I did not have a warm relationship with my father, so it was much easier to handle.

Eileen: When my mom passed, I felt I was living with a huge hole in every moment of my life, both waking and sleeping. It was hard to adjust to moving about with such an enormous hole.

When my dad passed two years later, the fact that I believed they were together again in heaven diminished the hole in me but tore away the entire feeling that I was part of a family unit. Now it was me here and them there. Pure and simple. I could no longer hope or hold onto either of them in this world.

Susan: Losing my parents at a young age is an experience that defies comparison. They were more than just guardians; they were the foundation of my existence, the tangible proof of my lineage and identity. Their absence leaves me grappling with disbelief, a persistent ache that never wanes. The sequence of their departure is an odd journey: My father died when I was 45, succumbing to cancer at the age of 77, followed by my mother six years later when I was 51 after a fierce 14-year struggle with leukemia. Despite their age, they exuded vitality until illness ravaged their bodies, leaving me to witness their gradual disintegration. It was heartbreaking on every level.

Theresa: I lost my mother when I was 17, and I lost my father when I was 36. My reactions to each death were diametrically opposed. I was scared when my mother died. I was relieved when my father passed. Sadly, I wasn't emotionally close to them when each died. With my mother, it was because I was a teenager and, as teenagers do, I wanted nothing to do with her. With my father, it was because he was a narcissist who had little room for anyone else.

My relationship with my father was very strained from the time I hit puberty, and at the same time, my mother was diagnosed with pulmonary fibrosis. When she died four years later, my father fell apart. He became the ultimate victim; he'd cry every night over his four or five cocktails. Poor him. He was alone. His wife died. He had no empathy for his daughter. I was there to take care of him. I cleaned his house and made him dinner every night. Dinner that he often complained about. Month after month after month.

I didn't mourn his passing; I felt free. After his funeral, I barely remembered that he had died because I had had so little contact with him since I had moved out of the house to go to college when I was 17.

J. J.: There are a lot of differences in losing my parents. The first one, I had more time to prepare, knowing that her illness and challenges were probably going to shorten her life expectancy and feeling like I was somewhat prepared although I certainly wasn't. She went much sooner than I thought.

When my father passed away about five years later, it was profound. Not just because I was daddy's little girl or because he had all of his mental awareness about him and his body just stopped, but because it truly left me an orphan. I had lost my only sibling before I lost either one of my parents, so the passing of my father was my last sense of my immediate family, and it hit hard.

Marly: I lost my mom when I was three years old. Not having her was a void that was never filled. I imagined how my life would be if she had lived; I romanticized how that would be.

When my dad died, I was 28 and we had a strained relationship. However, I felt a sudden sense of absolute aloneness knowing that I had NO parents. I remember thinking, "Now I'm an orphan."

2. How Did Losing Both Parents Affect You? What Feelings Initially Came Up?

James: My mother died almost 20 years before my father. And I wasn't with her when she died. I had gone through so much more by the time my father died, and he was 91, as opposed to my mother who was only 70. So, my shock was less profound. I had experience with death. But, still, my father had "taken care of me all through his life." I wondered, if worse comes to worse, who will take care of me? Not my sister, daughter, or friends. I am on my own. A girlfriend or significant other is not necessarily forever. Blood is. And now the source is gone.

Shyrl: I called my father, who died last, at least twice a day for a year and visited him when I could. He remarried a couple of years after my mother's death, a younger woman who was willing to care for him, so I was relieved of much of the responsibility that I would have felt obligated to fulfill otherwise. My main concern that he wouldn't be alone was allayed.

Kimberly: It's been 11 years now and I've remarried. My kids are now young adults, but I still feel orphaned in that I don't have my parents. And when I see my friends with their parents, I feel happy for them, but I also feel like I'm missing out. I try not to be jealous, but I say to my friends, 'Gosh, you are so lucky. Do you know how blessed you are to still have your parents?' They look at me like they do, but I know they don't think about it in the same way I do. I will always wish I had more time with my parents.

Linda: I was surprised at how hard it was, but it was the longest relationship I'd had in my life, and the time I spent filled so much of my time that I wasn't sure what to do with myself for a while. It also felt like there was no one ahead of me on the escalator going up anymore, and that was weird. As I enter my 70s, my dad's generation is all gone now in our family and with most of my friends as well. Also, it somehow felt like I was losing my mom again. It's hard to explain, but knowing they were side by side again just made me feel the loss again.

Judy: Being orphaned as an adult—meaning that moment you don't have a mommy and daddy—three things happened: there was a sense of loss, a feeling of freedom, and a new responsibility.

The loss was missing the ability to talk and go to my parents for guidance. The freedom was no longer having to worry about their opinions of what I did, which was always a concern no matter how old I got. And the responsibility was now my turn to walk in their shoes and be a representative of my parents. I'll go forward and be an example of the person they raised and make their memory and legacy proud.

Michael: Beyond the usual feelings of mourning and loss, what came up for me was the loss of a connection to my cultural past, as my mother spoke her parents' native Sicilian language. She was the last person I knew who could speak it and, with that and other cultural connections I learned from her, like cooking. So much ended when my last parent died. I felt unmoored and sent adrift.

Annette: As an only child, everything fell on me at a time when I had two young children to care for. The physical job of dealing with sorting through a home, possessions, and financial matters was overwhelming. I was in my late 20s and had no guidance on how to handle this tremendous burden.

Eileen: Ugh. This is a journey I do not wish upon anyone, yet it is one that will change your life. The experience will be different for each person, with far too many one step forward and one step back moments.

For me, a series of five severe losses in a row sent me to the depths that only a spiritual journey could start to bring me out of. My beliefs, which I know were always there, are much more concrete now.

I watched a conversation on grief between Stephen Colbert and Anderson Cooper. Colbert said that the loss of his father and brother was something he was thankful for because it taught him so much. It was a gift. "I felt thankful" was an odd viewpoint to take. I wish I had gained my newfound wisdom in a far less painful way.

Susan: Throughout my life, my parents were always there. I shared every triumph and tribulation with them, from childhood escapades to the founding of my own company—a tribute to my maternal heritage and my parents' shared entrepreneurial spirit. Their unwavering support fueled my ambitions. Yet, their absence loomed large, a void that seemed impossible to fill.

Theresa: Initially, I had a deep knowing that everything had changed and that nothing would be the same. I started a journal that night and wrote that my mom wouldn't be there when I graduated from high school or college or when I got married. It was a quiet knowing that I didn't talk about. And I remember feeling numb. In the first few days, I had to get busy and pick out my mother's casket, choose her outfit, and meet with the funeral director. My father was too distraught to handle these details.

I knew I was on my own and had no safe place to land after my mother died. I didn't even think about how that felt or what it meant. I had learned to be a little independent in the years leading to her death: she had been in and out of the hospital for four years, beginning when I was 13. I had a lot of mixed feelings about that. No one talked to me to tell me what was going on, and I didn't think she was seriously ill.

During her illness and after she died, I had to take on the responsibilities of grocery shopping, cooking, and cleaning for my father, along with taking care of him. I didn't like any of it. He would criticize my efforts. As strange as it seems, 50 years later, I still have a little anxiety when going into a grocery store, worried that I won't get the right thing or make it the right way.

So, I guess the feelings that came up were numbness, followed by resentment. I didn't resent her; I resented my father. My life after my mother's death held little joy. Now, in thinking about him and his passing, I mostly feel sorry for him. He was so miserable.

J. J.: That feeling of realizing that everything you knew about growing up was gone, everything that you couldn't remember, you could no longer reach out to your mom or dad and find an answer for. No one that truly knew everything about you from the day you were born. It felt heavy more than it felt sad. I felt a little lost, like I wasn't sure where I belonged.

Marly: Losing my mom as a toddler forever altered my life. It left an empty place forever in my heart. I mourn her and the life we could have had.

With my dad's death, even though we were not close, I was sad in a strange way. Sad that we didn't have a better relationship. Sad that he made poor health choices that caused him to die alone in a veteran's hospital. I think I finally forgave him for not being a good father—for not being the dad I needed.

3. Did it Change Your Inside World (e.g., Identity, Fear of Death, etc.)?

James: Yes. Imperceptibly. I had to become a different me. In the short term, I was shaken. And at the same time, in the case of my father, maybe liberated a little. I was no longer the son. I was a man without oversight. (My father was never short on advice or opinions, many of which I respected, most of which I did not necessarily share.)

My mother led me to believe I could do anything. My father led me to believe that the world was a dangerous place, and if I wasn't careful, something awful would happen. (My mother escaped the Nazis, and my father lived through Nazi occupation and then escaped from behind the Iron Curtain under Communism.)

Shyrl: I am an only child and sadly did not have much of a relationship with my parents past my teenage years when I came out and was disowned by them. But I always tried to show them love, despite them showing it to me "in their own way." I always wondered whether it would be harder to lose your parents if you were really close to them and had family ties, or if it would be harder to lose them when there are unresolved issues and painful memories.

The truth is, I don't know the answer to that question.

Kimberly: I went from feeling like part of a family and my identity as a daughter—I mean, I'm still technically a daughter, I just don't have parents anymore—so I'm not part of the familial relationship. I am the parent, and I have kids now. I do feel like it changed my identity in that I feel more alone. I don't feel like I have an emotional support network around me, like parents are, but what can you do? I have to keep going. I tend to focus more on being that for my kids.

My sense of mortality also came into greater focus. I thought about it since the age of eight or so; when you start thinking ahead, you realize people die. That means your parents are going to die someday—that you are going to die someday. I thought about it as a kid, but when you lose your parents, it brings it back up again in all its ugliness.

I don't worry about when I die or what's going to happen to me, as much as I do worry about what will happen to my kids. I started thinking about the responsibility of that and how necessary it is to have my affairs in order, like my parents did for me. And besides a trust and will, I bought life insurance in addition to whatever assets

I have so that there will be extra for my loved ones to help the transition when I do pass.

Linda: I think it did affect many parts of my interior world. I consider mortality more now. My dreams have been exceeded by my immediate family, so my dreams for the future are simply not to be a burden to them as we age. Life is a bit harder for them, and we don't want to add stress. I now focus on how to stay healthy and think about what we want to do with the time we have.

Judy: The loss of my second parent, my father, reawakened the grief of losing my mother. I was busy looking after my dad after her loss and worrying about the family, and I didn't fully acknowledge my grief until I lost him six years later.

Michael: After my last parent died, I felt as though I was orphaned. Also, my sense of mortality became very real. My dad died at 70. His father died at 70. I just turned 70, although each generation seems to look and feel much younger. Still... there it is.

Annette: I struggled through all this, made a lot of mistakes, and put a lot of stress on my relationship with my husband. Ultimately, I learned a lot and grew stronger because of it.

Eileen: When my mother passed away, I looked out upon the world often and thought, 'How do people go on without a mother? How are we supposed to do this?" When my father passed away, the looking outward retreated to looking inward. "Now I am doing this on my own," I realized.

Susan: In my heart, my mother and father remain champions whom I can no longer turn to for guidance. I sometimes find solace in imaginary conversations—asking my father for lucky lottery numbers or seeking strength from my mother. Yet, the numbers remain elusive, and their voices are but echoes in the void.

Theresa: When I lost my mother, I was a lost girl. I mourned her. I was terrified because I was stuck with a father who didn't think all that much of me and who believed his needs were more important. I worried about how I would ever get by. My brother had moved out of the house years before, and though we would talk occasionally, I was alone with my father.

I learned to rely on my friends, though I never talked much about what was going on. I didn't want to be the girl in school whose mother had died. I was heartbroken deep down inside with a veneer of "everything's fine."

J. J.: The biggest internal change for me and my identity was not having that sense of belonging. It hurt not having those people I knew had my back—no matter what—I could turn to. It threw my life in a blender, mixed it all up, and made a big mess for myself.

I was young enough to still be working and have a sense of purpose every day. I had an identity at work and identified myself by my career. That helped.

But when someone asked me where my parents were, it was a heavy cloud for a long time to find a way to say I didn't have any. One thing that changed for me was a commitment and passion to live my best life every day, savor every memory, and do things I kept putting off until tomorrow.

I wanted to continue to make my parents proud, and every time something magnificent happened, or I'd get a promotion to be able to buy a new home or whatever, I would often walk over to the phone to call them and then realize I couldn't. It's very strange when you have to learn to pat yourself on the back because your parents aren't doing it anymore.

4. Did it Change Your Outside World (e.g., Family Unit, Friendships, Career, etc.)?.

James: My outside world? No. Not really. Except for the inheritance, which was enough to provide some stability I had not had before. Long term, not really. Now that I am in my late 60s, most of the changes have been internal. These changes are related to my upbringing that I have worked on to understand, forgive, be grateful for, and heal and adjust, which has changed my outside world in the way I interact with people—for the better.

Shyrl: My outside world didn't change; my circumstances were the same. I always felt on my own, so not having them around was a feeling I was familiar with. I had lost them long before, although after my mother's death, my father found he needed me much more, and he made an effort to be more understanding and tolerant.

Linda: It changed my immediate family. When my father died, my stepmother of 30-plus years decided she didn't need us anymore. While she was always difficult, she made sure I was there to help every step of the way with my father and was the only grandma my kids had, so her actions were doubly hurtful.

It made me realize that if you don't have trust in your relationships or feel safe, then they are better left by the wayside. Life is truly precious.

Michael: I have lived away from my family for almost 40 years. It didn't change my outside world in that I had already created my own life here in California. Going back home to New York, however, will never be the same.

Like the Thomas Wolfe novel says, "You can never go home again." I felt that. The nostalgia for the place I grew up was strong. A deep missing of that, like another loss.

Annette: In the short term, it did change my world. There was so much to process and adjust to. It was a rough period for me as my dad passed only one year after my mom.

Eileen: The effects on my outside world will be continuous: the questions I forgot to ask, the stories I needed to clarify, the advice that is no longer there, and the comfort of knowing someone who knows me and cares about me.

Getting to do nice things for them because they would enjoy it—that's the part of grief that never goes away. It's the connection of having had a relationship.

Susan: As a mother myself, I keenly feel my mother and father's absence, mourning the love they would have showered upon my children. It's a pain that cuts deep, a reminder of all that could have been.

Theresa: My family structure was never the same. Looking back, I do know that I loved my mother and that she loved me, and we were victims of bad timing. I like to think that had she lived, we would have become very close, like we were when I was younger. Though

I'm grateful for my life, romances, career, and friends, I wonder how it would have been different had she lived.

Luckily for me, my father started dating soon after my mother's death in February 1974. By October, he married a woman he met through the parish priest. Shortly after his marriage, he made it clear that there wasn't room for me in the new family. His new wife had an 11-year-old daughter, whom my father adopted.

During the summer breaks in college, he told me it would be best if I could find somewhere else to live until I returned to school. I became driven to achieve because I knew I couldn't go home again. I excelled in college and worked at two jobs after I graduated. I was very lucky that through various job opportunities, I wound up with a fun, highly rewarding career in television with many accolades, including awards for investigative journalism and production.

J. J.: It changed my outside world in the sense that people who had maybe been a little bit distant, like cousins or even aunts and uncles, suddenly became a part of my world. I have always been blessed to have friendships that truly were my chosen family, but I came to rely on them in a way that I certainly never had before.

5. What Steps Helped You the Most in Moving Forward Through Your Grief?

James: Therapy. I didn't go into therapy to deal with the loss of my parents. But as I cleared away the debris of the past, I found a lot of source material in those relationships.

Shyrl: To move forward in my life after their death, it was important for me not to wallow in regrets about a life I couldn't change. I made an effort not to be consumed with all the what-ifs because it just doesn't matter.

The most important thing I did was to forgive them and embrace what they had given me, which is a strong work ethic, a strong moral compass, and a desire to do the right thing by demonstrating love, kindness, and nonjudgment while I made my way in the world.

Kimberly: I threw myself into motherhood because my young kids were all I had. I also had a unique situation due to my divorce where I had 50/50 custody with their dad, so I'd have them for a week, then they'd be gone for a week with my ex. When they were with me, I was a full-time mom, 100 percent focused on them and their needs, and then in my off time every other week, I could focus on myself—work out, socialize, and go to therapy, so I got time to work on myself.

If I had just been a mom and focused on my kids, it would have been harder for me to work on myself. I just kept moving forward. I didn't stop or stagnate. I kept balancing life with my children, and that was such a blessing.

Linda: At my age, sadly, I am in good company, as most of my friends are experiencing the same with their parents: caring for them, dementia, disease, and then loss. We support each other. Also, when attending so many of my friends' parents' funerals, I realized I only knew them a little and not who they were.

I look at people differently. I listen to them more, ask more, and really try to know them better.

Judy: That kid inside you will always be there. And then you have to step in and be the parent to the kid. It's an odd thing that happens.

And then you look around and realize, as odd and painful as it is, this is all a part of life.

Any time you are taken away from your parents—at any stage in life—I don't think you can ever avoid feeling exactly how that felt as a child. Ever.

Michael: It's been three years and I'm not sure if I've made much progress moving forward. I remain in mourning. There are good days and bad days. Having a friend who can sit and listen, where I can share stories of the good times, does seem to help a little. Sometimes just being with someone in silence can feel comforting.

Annette: I felt a huge void and emptiness in my life despite having my own close immediate family with my husband. We decided to have our third child, with our youngest being seven at the time. That gave me a new purpose in life and a different outlook for the future.

Eileen: Grief is a full-out recovery process. I chipped off two to three percent of the pain from every single thing I used to soothe my pain: every book I read, classes taken, podcasts, quotes, YouTube, travel, walks, planting flowers, talking with friends, managing my finances, self-care, old photos, crystals, herbs, reputable mediums, lighting candles in remembrance. In the end, time does not heal—it just solidifies that your new life is now a reality.

Of course, this doesn't mention the many weeks of not eating, not sleeping, sleeping too much, not keeping up with all the to-dos, or the feeling of being totally without direction. And the tears that would suddenly, without warning, pour forth.

Susan: Early on, I was in such disbelief that the heroes who made me were gone; it took a few years to sink in. Talking to them, saying an evening prayer for them, and telling my own children stories about them made it a little easier.

I can't help but hold tight to my daughters' faces and imagine how my parents would have adored them. I ask for them every day. I ask for a sign, a symbol, and whisper in the wind—any tiny gesture from them.

Theresa: I tried to be with my friends as much as possible. I also think I was forced at an early age to test the boundaries and turn inward to find the fortitude on how to move forward. I suppose I could have collapsed and fallen apart after my mother's death, but I doubled down and became stronger. I didn't feel as though I had a choice. I was lucky to meet people along the way who provided guidance. I think of them as my guardian angels sent by my mother. Each time I had contact with my father in subsequent years was a reminder that I was on my own.

I don't think I began to heal from grief until I was about 40. Before that, I didn't have enough distance from my mother's death and my father's rejection. It didn't feel safe for me to stop working, pushing and trying to figure out how to live on my own. It didn't feel safe to stop to reflect on what had happened. It seemed more important to me to have a strong facade.

Now, of course, looking back, I see that I started drinking in my teens to self-medicate and I was often depressed. But I didn't connect what happened with the way I was feeling. Only when I entered a deep depression and started therapy did I begin to heal. Forgiving my father was a turning point for me—it felt like I was finally releasing the burden of carrying him around in my mind.

J. J.: I'm not sure I specifically took steps that moved me forward. I just got out of bed every day and went through the motions of living the life I'd always known. The greatest gift I could rely on was the fact that all of my close friends knew my parents, had been to our house for dinners or holidays—my dad joining us to go camping, my mother joining us for happy hour—they knew them, and they knew them as adults when we were adults.

Being able to share those memories—and knowing they knew who I was talking about and had a sense of them and could also share their memories about them—helped me a great deal. It kept them present in my everyday life, and the hole inside me eventually got smaller and smaller.

Marly: It was easier for me to move forward knowing I did the best I could in the relationship with my father. I did nothing wrong; my dad was alone because of his choices. It was not my fault.

6. Do You Celebrate Holidays and Special Occasions Differently Now? Did The Loss of Your Parents Change Your Family Dynamics?

James: Yes. Now it's all about my grandson. I celebrate with my daughter and her family, but other holidays, like Mother's Day or Father's Day, I just remember my parents. I pay homage to them in whatever way seems appropriate.

Shyrl: We never celebrated holidays, so I didn't have to mourn the loss of family traditions.

Kimberly: Holidays were a very lonesome time for me. With my mom and dad, we were such a small family—it was the three of us—and holidays were important to us. When they were gone, it became even more important for me to spend time with my kids and maximize holiday time. I didn't have them every holiday and was alone on many holidays.

I'm very grateful to my network of friends who would invite me over and take me in, but I did feel kind of lonely. Very alone. I didn't have my parents or anywhere to go. I didn't know from one holiday to the next where I'd be celebrating a holiday or with whom.

It's better now that I'm married, but holidays are still tough. I try to fill them with friends—friends are the family you choose. I'm always welcoming to friends and my husband's family.

Linda: Our holidays are now centered on our kids and grandkids. I miss my parents a lot, though. I think that's natural and to be expected.

Judy: My mom was an incredibly strong woman—even a little feared as the matriarch. Her absence gave everyone the opportunity to step away from the family routine that she had always dictated, and maybe start in a new way. All my siblings had family, but I did not, so there were many changes as we adapted to the new family structure.

My siblings started doing things as the head parent now to their kids in the absence of our mother telling us what to do as their mother. So, it did shift things. We have a huge family, and I'm sure we'd still have those big family gatherings if my parents were still alive, but things just fell into place after the loss of them both.

Michael: For the Christmas holidays, I like to cook foods that I remember my grandmother—who loved me unconditionally—and later my mother made. Sadly, my only family left is a sibling who lives on the other side of the country, and my friends are not familiar with my cultural traditions.

Sharing is the best way for me to celebrate home in my heart and honor my past, so when I can, I will.

Annette: Not really. Holiday celebrations continued with, and for, my children, my husband, and his extended family.

Eileen: I don't celebrate holidays any longer. My parents' passing took the pressure off of family obligations. And rather than being a week (or weeks) of preparation, the single holiday day comes and goes gently. I accept invitations to attend meals with others, but the idea of holding or building traditions into the future has stopped.

In a way, history-making stopped when my parents passed. Now, I pay more attention to the spiritual aspects of the holidays.

Susan: In the past, I had not spent holidays with my siblings, which was not obligatory. I now jump on planes and cars to visit them on most holidays. Recently, I returned to my home state of Michigan to spend the 4th of July with my sister. It was the first time I was back in the state where I grew up and where I suffered the tremendous loss of both my parents.

It was an odd feeling. I enjoy reconnecting with family, as their faces remind me of my parents, and their passed-on mannerisms make me smile. Talking about what they might know truly helps. It's all I have now, and it's all I can give to my kids. Some stories are wildly fun to recall.

Theresa: I used to celebrate holidays with my husband, older brother, and his wife. It felt normal, safe, and fun. When I got divorced after nine years, I would still go to my brother's house. However, when my brother died 11 years ago, I was on my own. At first, I'd start to panic a little beginning in August about what I would do for Thanksgiving, which is the holiday I like best.

As the years have passed, I've relaxed quite a bit. Friends have come and gone—I live in the transient city of Washington, D.C., so there's no one group I celebrate with. If I don't have plans, if I haven't been invited anywhere, I'm fine. It is just another day, after all. But I don't go on Facebook from before Thanksgiving to two weeks after because all the happy pictures make me feel a little sorry for myself.

J. J.: I think anyone who has suffered a loss realizes that the first of everything, first Christmas, first birthday, Mother's Day, Father's Day, you name it, is significantly different. I set out on a path after I lost my father not to follow my traditions, not to replicate what I knew I couldn't, so I usually went away, as if the pain wouldn't follow me wherever I was going, but it did somehow make it a touch softer.

Two or three years later, I started incorporating the traditions into my life with my partner and my friends. To this day, I still toast every single one of them at Christmas dinner or my birthday. I celebrate their birthday doing what I know they would want to do on their birthday, and it brings me comfort.

Marly: Losing my mom so young and having a dad who had no family, we didn't have any real holiday traditions. I have tried to make my children's lives better than what I had, but we still don't follow traditional holidays.

We choose to celebrate each other.

7. What Words or Advice Were Most Comfort to You in The Early Days After Your Loss?

James: Take one day at a time. Sometimes one minute.

Shyrl: My friends were kind and supportive of me when my parents died, but I made an effort to keep my very conflicted feelings and emotions in check. My relationship with my parents was so different than what my friends had with theirs, but I took their efforts at consoling me as great kindness. No one knew my parents, so it wasn't personal.

Kimberly: Not many of my friends had experienced the loss of their parents, so there weren't really any words of advice. It's funny, people just don't know what to say to you when you've lost someone. Most people told me that they cared and were there for me, but I was left without words of wisdom and left alone to figure it out for myself.

I didn't really read any books or seek outside help back then, I just waded through it on my own. It's hard. I really didn't have a lot of input. I understand if people don't know what to say, but it can feel like they don't care when they say nothing. I'm sure that's not the case, but that's how so many who are grieving tend to internalize it.

Linda: I think being around people who understood helped, being allowed to feel sad when it cropped up, or being free to talk about memories and laugh with people who knew my dad.

Judy: I grew to have a close relationship with my parents, and luckily for me, my friends all knew my parents. I can't think of anything that helps you more than having people in your life—outside your family, *your* people—who actually knew your parents. You then get to talk about them, relive special memories, and don't lose them the same way as a result. They get to live. That is such a healing comfort.

In my life, I take every opportunity to meet my friends' parents—it's so important. Their parents will be gone someday, and we will talk about them. They will need to hear these stories, and they will bring happiness and comfort to both of us when we share them. People just don't realize how important that is.

Michael: I don't think there was anything that could comfort me when my last parent died. I felt tremendously alone. In time, having friends check in to show they cared was everything. Especially months and years later, when it seems like the world just moves on.

Annette: Don't rush things if you don't feel ready.

Eileen: The book *Healing After the Loss of Your Mother: A Grief & Comfort Manual* by Elaine Mallon helped me.

I asked friends to take a walk with me on the anniversary of my mom's passing.

I intentionally travel to places I remember my dad talking about visiting and enjoying, like the Isle of Skye in Scotland.

When my dog passed away, neighbors came by to express their condolences. They sent cards and came by to talk. I was honest with them about how much it hurt to lose my dog and they, in turn, cried in front of me. I am aware that I used talking about my dog to heal my grief about my mom and then my dad. I found people would weep and express emotions over a dog more easily than the discomfort of talking about losing a parent.

Susan: Sharing memories. I found—and continue to find—solace in memories of their dedication and humor, my father's wit contrasting with my mother's steadfastness.

Theresa: This is going to sound so strange, but in the early days, there weren't words, deeds, or advice. I was 17, determined to look like everything was fine. I was incapable of having a deep emotional conversation. When people at the funeral said, "I'm so sorry," I'd smile and say, "Thanks so much." And then I'd make a little joke.

Decades later, therapy was the most helpful. Through it, and through spiritual practice, I was able to forgive my father and realize that I wasn't a terrible person to my mother. I was able to forgive myself too. I wasn't very kind to her as a kid, and it's one of my regrets. Dealing with both issues are two of the accomplishments of which I'm most proud.

J. J.: I was very comforted to know I had friends who loved me and that they would be there when I stopped grieving, when I stopped wanting to be in bed, and when I stopped crying at every love song that came on the radio. I knew they would be there throughout my entire process, and that's probably the greatest gift I could've ever had because I knew I wasn't alone even though I felt alone.

Marly: There were no words that could have helped. I was in my late twenties; I didn't know anyone—aside from my sister—who had already lost both parents, so no friends were able to understand the "adult orphan" feeling. It felt very lonely.

8. What words, deeds, or advice did *not* help you?

James: Nobody wants to hear, "You'll get over it." In my case, I was most irritated by my sibling's inability to deal with either one of my parents' deaths and suggested that "our parents would want us to do this or that." People telling you what your dead parents would want or pretty much any sentence that contains the words "you should" sets my teeth on edge.

Shyrl: The only thing that irritated me was when people would use my loss as an opportunity to talk about themselves without any regard for my feelings.

Kimberly: I had a close friend who's very empathic and who knew my parents well, but he did not show up for my father's or my mother's memorial. I was so disappointed and hurt. I later asked him why he didn't attend. He just said he felt uncomfortable and just couldn't.

I told him I understood that death is uncomfortable, but he really let me down. In that situation, it wasn't about *him*. It was about *me*, and I needed friends to emotionally support me. Do you want to know who's most uncomfortable with death? The person who just lost a person they loved dearly.

Linda: Anytime someone says it will get better in time or stuff along those lines, it does not help. I think the best thing someone can do for another is to be a good listener. Validate their feelings.

Annette: "I understand what you're going through." Unless you've gone through it yourself, you can't possibly understand!

Eileen: I react terribly to the words, "Our thoughts and prayers are with you." Those words can be uttered without an ounce of true empathy for or understanding of debilitating personal loss. That phrase is cruelly overused.

I also found myself reacting strongly when a sibling's brother-in-law asked my brother, after my mother's passing, "So tell me who your mother was?" I felt it was invasive and of trite curiosity. If that person hadn't taken the time to know my mother in her lifetime, then he didn't deserve to know her after. Apparently, I had some anger to work through.

I also dislike the words, "Well, she was old," and "At least her suffering has stopped." It's like throwing away a person. Of course, she was old, and, of course, she suffered—this is life. And she was my *mom*.

Theresa: Being alone without any emotional support, especially at such a young age. But being so young, I didn't even *know* I needed emotional support. I wasn't sitting there thinking, "Why don't I have anyone to help me?" I didn't expect it, so I wasn't disappointed it was missing.

Looking at it now, 50 years later, I do see a girl who I'm pretty darn proud of. She made her way despite all that was missing.

J. J.: There is one specific scenario that sticks out for me. My father suffered a stroke and wasn't given long to live but was doing so well, and I committed to spending as much time as possible being present in the moment and enjoying him. When he passed, I returned to work and someone said to me, "Well, it's not like you didn't see it coming, right?" As if knowing that someone is sick and their life is going to be shortened helps eliminate any pain? That was so ridiculous, and it actually made me angry. I had to walk out of the room.

I'm not sure why or how but I was able to give a lot of people grace because they just don't know what to say when this happens. There isn't anything anybody can say that makes the pain go away, but having friends telling me they love me, showing up, and being there for me helped the time pass. I certainly didn't surround myself with anyone who couldn't understand what I was going through.

9. How Long Did it Take to Regain Some Sense of "Normalcy" Again?

James: That's hard to say. I think when you lose both your parents, you go numb for a while. And if you're involved in something like a new job, marriage, relationship, or something that keeps you extra busy for good reason, you lose track of time. Cleaning up issues of an estate can also numb you.

If I had to guess, I'd say a year. At least.

Shyrl: I have tried to remind myself of the good memories I had as a child with my extraordinary parents; I think I have created a happier outcome for myself by understanding their limitations and accepting them even as they were unable or unwilling to accept mine.

In some ways, I think I have created a normalcy I never had with them while they were alive.

Kimberly: Do we ever? I mean, when we lose our parents, do we ever regain a sense of normality? The fact is things are not normal or the same after. Life as you knew it is irrevocably changed and different simply by the mere fact that your parents are gone. I had to quickly pull myself up by my bootstraps so my kids had someone there for them.

It took at least a year or more. Eleven years later, I wouldn't say I'm totally over it. There are still times when I want to call my mom, ask her about simple things like recipes. That never really goes away but it lessens... but it never goes away.

Linda: I'm not even sure what "normal" even is anymore. There is an unfillable void, which is the new normal. Time does help with the adjustment.

Judy: For me, it took a good three years to feel through each loss. I found the first year, regardless, was just devastating. The second year has so many ups and downs; it's just a roller coaster ride. By year three, things settled in, and I hit my "new normal." And then you handle the feelings differently.

I just thought the other day, "Gosh, I really miss my parents." I don't think about it a lot, but it still hits from time to time, even 28 years later.

Michael: With my father, who died decades ago, I was devastated, and his loss still reverberates. But I eased back into my life more easily than with the passing of my mother. It's been three years, and I'm still not there. I just feel there's so much more to mourn when both parents die.

Annette: Finding a renewed sense of purpose and something to look forward to helped me the most. Being pregnant again gave me a whole new outlook on my life, so it was relatively easy to establish my "new normal."

Eileen: There is no return to previous normalcy; it becomes a new normal.

The grief has changed over time. I often find myself thinking, "Mom would have liked doing this," or "Dad would have loved this view." Instead of continuing to well up and cry over the loss, I gracefully take a moment and imagine that they are indeed there with me. It brings me comfort and allows me to appreciate the small moments.

Susan: I would never say I have healed the wound of losing them, but I have coated it with the joy of being brought up by them, and I am comforted daily by piecing together the goodness and the indestructible qualities that have made me a better person.

I was raised by good people, so I honor them by passing along something good almost every day.

Theresa: It was never a "normal" life, so I had to create my own version. There is a distinct "before" and "after" her death. I did find happiness and love, but not from my father. There is no "before and after," with my father with one exception: When my father got sick and was in the hospital, I made a decision. I was about 34, and I had a spiritual moment of grace when I felt God tell me that I had done everything I could do for him, and if I never saw him again, I would not feel guilty when he died. He died two years later.

"Grace" is the only way I can describe it. I had a sense and belief that I had done all I could to have a relationship with him, but ultimately, I couldn't control him, and I couldn't make him love me or even be kind. I made peace with that. So "before" my moment of grace, I carried a lot of anger. "After," I felt relieved. That moment was a real gift in my life. Huge. When friends now ask how to deal with death, I say: "Do everything you need to do so that you won't feel guilty if they die tomorrow. That's all you need to do."

I finally, FINALLY did forgive my father. I was about 45 and had been praying about it and working on it with my therapist. One afternoon, sitting at the beach, I thoroughly embraced the thought he did the best he could do and he couldn't give what he didn't have. Though it was simple, it felt very profound. My life felt much lighter after that wave of awareness broke over me.

J. J.: I think I gained a sense of normalcy pretty quickly, but there was nothing normal about it. It's a new normal when you realize you're on your own, in my case, my entire family was gone, so it's not the normal I ever knew and I just told myself, "Well, I guess this is the new normal. This is normal, but it may not be normal to others. It's my normal and I had to find a way to be okay with that and pulled the strength that both my parents gave me to know I could do anything I set my mind to.

Marly: My everyday life continued on normally; I lived three thousand miles away from my dad at the time of his death and our relationship was strained, so my life didn't change much. In some ways, it was a relief and closure to a chapter. I was able to move forward and forgive.

I finally took a moment to reflect on my life and felt thankful for the few good things my father taught me. He instilled in me a good work ethic, a love for reading, and the importance of being respectful and polite to others. He also emphasized the need not to pass judgment on others who may be fighting battles we don't know about.

I chose to move forward in peace, and without resentments, guilt, or regrets.

10. Any Words of Advice For Someone Newly Going Through Double Parental Loss?

James: All I can offer is my experience, not my advice. In my experience, you learn to honor your feelings and identify them as best you can but not be swallowed up by them. Losing yourself in something else is getting lost, not moving toward resolution. You're going to feel it. Pain. Exhaustion. Maybe relief. It depends on your relationship with your parent(s).

But, again, these are the people who are the source of your being. So, there is something inarguably profound that is worth paying attention to.

Shyrl: Grief will bring up abandonment issues, memories of both happiness and sadness, and many regrets. Don't lose yourself in the past, whether it was happy or painful. Instead, believe you were once loved and treasured and are worthy of love and of loving now.

Kimberly: Go easy on yourself. If your friends don't know how to show support, tell them. Be honest about your needs. Accept help. Take time for yourself: yoga, therapy, working out, eating well, and socializing when you can. You'll see life does go on, so go on with it. See the value in your life, make it exciting, and if you can, be a beacon of love for others.

Linda: Don't put any expectations on yourself. Just let whatever comes up roll over you. There will be times when you'll be driving along or observing something, and it just hits you. Let it flow.

I found comfort sleeping with the blanket my dad used in his last days for months. Do whatever works—whatever gives you the comfort you need.

Judy: I think you move forward in the time that it takes you to move forward. Keep it simple. If you're fearful of the pain or the pain is too much for you, distract yourself for a little while. But if you have the courage to sit with the feelings—because they are the storm that creates the rainbow—then missing someone becomes the most beautiful part of loving them.

Let yourself go through it and give yourself grace.

Michael: If you had a difficult relationship with either parent, you will still grieve. That's natural. When I came out to my parents as a young adult, my Sicilian, strict Roman Catholic parents could not accept it. I didn't want to be condemned, so I moved to the opposite coast and only visited on holidays. Alone.

What helps me now is to remember the version of my parents who loved me as a child. I reminisce about the times when I was a happy kid in New York, about the times my mother took me shopping or to get her hair done on Fifth Avenue at five years old. Or when my dad would take his wide-eyed little boy to the Museum of Natural History. I focus on the good memories because they still make me smile.

Annette: Take things slowly: day by day, week by week. It's okay to be angry or mad at the world. It's okay to feel sad and have a bad day. It will get easier!

Eileen: Do grief your way. In your time. Give grief space to expand and then settle. Let it move through you. Let the tears flow; they will stop eventually. Approach grief with slow honesty. Avoid expectations of yourself and others; very little will unfold as you expected.

When you become overwhelmed, remove yourself for some quiet time. At other times, it is best to keep your mind busy with a project or a good walk in nature. Find still moments and listen to your intuition. There is guidance available to us daily.

Susan: This is what helped me in time: I find strength in my lineage, a legacy of resilience passed down through generations. Reflect on the good. Every day I carry their essence within me, a testament to their enduring influence.

Though they may no longer walk this earth, I believe they watch over me, their spirits buoyed by a newfound vitality, and I take comfort in the hope that they continue to find joy in their ethereal existence. Remember to live the life your parents gave you.

Theresa: There are great gifts to be found in grief. Even if you can't see them right now, they're there and they'll make themselves known with time if you keep yourself open to receiving them. I have empathy, which I didn't have before, an interest in what people are going through and a big-picture belief that death is another part of life. I'm not afraid of it.

Additionally, I know I can get through whatever may get thrown my way. I trust myself. I've often said that every year gets better, and that's still true for me. Once I graduated from college and got my first job, I realized I could make my own way. It was as if a light shone from above and a big weight lifted off my shoulders. I was making my own life safe. You can too, no matter what the circumstances.

J. J.: If you can, try to realize the incredible gift your parents gave you and your life and honor that gift by living it. It's absolutely true that healing takes time. The pain never goes away completely, but it will lessen.

The 'new normal' in time will become normal to you. It can be helpful to remember that you are their legacy so live your life well. Honor your parents while honoring the pain in the grief. Continue loving your parents and live to make them proud.

Marly: It doesn't matter how old you are when your parents die; whether you had a good or bad relationship, you feel a sense of loss. Maybe it's a loss of history. Maybe it's knowing the finality of the people who gave you life—who either supplied your DNA or gave birth to you from their heart—are gone.

While I'm not sure, it is all valid. We all share that core sense of loss when our parents are both gone. You are not alone in any of this.

Footprints to Follow

If you are struggling to find your way—or reaching for hope and resilience—talk to others who've been there. Share your story. Find comfort in the community of others who've walked this path and left emotional footprints to follow.

Find strength in yourself and in others. There's so much compassion out there when it comes to this experience.

If a hand reaches out to you, and you need it, don't be afraid to take it.

We are all in this together.

PART III: HOW TO SUPPORT SOMEONE WHO IS GRIEVING

"Too often we underestimate the power of a touch, a smile, a kind word, a listening ear, an honest compliment, or the smallest act of caring, all of which have the potential to turn a life around."

— Leo Buscaglia

CHAPTER 1

Comfort 101

IT IS DIFFICULT TO SEE someone we care about in emotional pain. After their second parent dies, your loved one most often is plunged into a depth of grief and isolation they've never felt before.

Myles, a successful business executive in his mid-50s with a happy marriage, two kids, and a loving extended family, was enjoying a happy life when his last parent died. He speaks for many of us who've lost both parents: *"I feel lost—like I'm orphaned now."*

Feeling vulnerable and alone after losing both parents are the most common reactions across gender, age, religious background, or position in life.

When we lose our only surviving parent, grief feels oddly unfamiliar because it involves so many added layers that directly impact the bereaved's internal and external worlds. After losing both parents, most say they thought the death of the first parent would have prepared them for the loss of the second.

Somehow, however, double parental loss is just "profoundly different." It's a life transition. A time of change, adaptation, soul-searching, *and* grief.

A person trying to comfort someone in grief must keep in mind that nothing you do or say can take your loved one's pain away. You can't cheer them out of it or magically make it all better. You can't "fix" them—because they're not broken—they're grieving.

It's an uncomfortable place to be as a supporter, but there are some basic steps you can take to help the one who's grieving.

SHOW UP

If you're ready to step up, it's important to clear the air and acknowledge any uneasiness you might feel. Focus on being present, and if your connection was crucial to the grieving before the death of their parent, it will be even more so now.

Please don't assume your presence, either physically or from a distance, will be a burden. There may be times when privacy is needed, but a personal crisis is not the time for the person struggling with loss to feel isolated or abandoned.

Grief is an unpredictable, gradual process that needs room to unfold. The simple act of "showing up" for the one grieving can have an incredible healing effect.

This means demonstrating that you care and acknowledge their heartache. It's signaling through words and actions that you are here for them now, in any way they need, for as long as they need you. Be sure to either tell them that directly or in some written form.

When we show up for someone, we demonstrate that we care, that we are reliable and committed.

If they need space at any time, invite them to tell you; assure them it will not hurt your feelings.

This period is about them.

Showing up means you are there *with them* and *for them*.

BE A GRIEF ALLY

You don't need to be a grief expert to know how to be a good human and a valuable grief ally. Just be authentic and lead with your heart. Four simple actions you can follow are:

- Be present
- Be patient
- Be a good listener
- Be reliable

Don't blame yourself if you don't know what to say or where to start. We don't live in a culture that teaches us how to cope with or support someone through grief until we go through it ourselves. So naturally, if we haven't experienced loss firsthand, it helps to educate ourselves or have someone with experience guide us.

Your desire to help is an incredible first step. When we're grieving, the security that comes with knowing we have someone we can count on, reassuring us that we are not alone, is of tremendous value.

Healing begins when someone is there alongside us to witness our pain.

You don't need to have answers, offer advice, or say and do all the right things. The most important thing you can do for a grieving person is to simply be there with an open heart, open ears, and open arms.

Bear Witness

Grief is best processed when it is acknowledged. And that can't be done in a state of isolation.

"Bearing witness" is a term used in grief recovery to describe the act of being there for the pain of another, of acknowledging the reality of it, and giving the person in grief permission to feel and express themselves fully.

"Each person's grief is as unique as their fingerprint. But what everyone has in common is that no matter how they grieve, they share a need for their grief to be witnessed," writes David Kessler in his book *Finding Meaning: The Sixth Stage of Grief.*[1]

"That doesn't mean needing someone to try to lessen it or reframe it for them. The need is for someone to be fully present to the magnitude of their loss without trying to point out the silver lining."

Holding Space

When you walk alongside someone in grief, allowing them to unburden their painful feelings without feeling inadequate, you help provide a place for them to express their deepest emotions.

This safe and sacred zone allows another to feel protected, seen, and heard. It is a place where you allow another to be human and real, where vulnerability is honored.

A transformative healing comes when someone is given room to fully express themselves, even completely fall apart, and know someone who cares will be there to lift them back up again.

We allow people to "die with dignity." The heartbroken deserve the space to "grieve with dignity" and without judgment as well.

This is why 'holding space' is such a sacred gift—to extend and receive.

GRIEF IS NOT A COMPETITION

It's sad to say, but many people, sometimes innocently and mindlessly, invalidate a person's grief by sharing their story about their experience with grief.

They tell their own tale of woe rather than fully allowing the one sharing to be heard. "Oh, you think that's bad…" they might say, as if it's a contest to see whose story is the most tragic or painful.

That kind of response can leave the person who originally shared feeling dismissed, minimized, unheard, exposed for being vulnerable, and ultimately irritated. They might even shut down entirely as a result.

So, remember:

- Listening shows respect.
- Sharing doesn't always need a response; it just needs to be acknowledged.
- Keep the focus on them, not you.
- Unless your story involves a similar loss, please don't share. Not now.
- Share what's relatable, but don't shift focus.
- Grief is not a competition where anyone wins.

There is a time and a place to talk about stories of loss, but comparisons are never helpful. The intention may be an attempt to connect, but that usually backfires. People quickly figure out with whom and where it's safe to share as a result.

When you are a grief ally, please keep in mind a person in deep grief isn't capable of being the best listener. Their mind is busy, and their nervous system is on edge. They're just trying to survive.

Your generous and caring focus needs to be on them right now.

Getting Started

To be the best supporter you can be, it is helpful to read and really understand Part I of this book, titled *The Adult Orphan*. It can be difficult to show true empathy if we don't understand the grief process or the full scope of how losing both parents can affect a person.

Once you get familiar with the emotions and cycles your loved one might experience, you will be better prepared to offer more compassion and guidance, especially if things get a little chaotic. "One step forward, two steps back" setbacks are common, and you'll be able to remind the one grieving that it's to be expected and okay.

You can be proud that you're one of the people who care enough to learn more.

Many readers of *Healing After the Loss of Your Mother: A Grief & Comfort Manual* said they read the book or listened to the audio version together with their partner in bed before going to sleep or with a friend on the couch with a hot cup of tea.

This kind of display provides that comforting sense that "we are in this together."

You can also give that a try with this book. (Or any other that works.)

Empathy

Empathy and compassion are the two pillars of effective grief support. While some confuse the actual meaning of each, it's good to know the subtle difference:

> **Empathy**: The action of understanding, being aware of, being sensitive to, and vicariously experiencing the feelings, thoughts, and experiences of another.[2]

A popular Brené Brown quote sums this up well: "Empathy is a strange and powerful thing. There is no script. There is no right way or wrong way to do it. It's simply listening, holding space, withholding judgment, emotionally connecting, and communicating that incredibly healing message of 'You're not alone.'"[3]

"Emotionally connecting" is key here. Empathy is the ability to relate by stepping into someone else's shoes and feeling the other person's emotions with them.

Compassion

Compassion, on the other hand, differs from empathy, in that it's about "recognizing" someone's suffering and wanting to help them. It's about care and action. More formally, the definition reads this way:

> **Compassion**: Sympathetic consciousness of others' distress together with a desire to alleviate it.[4]

In both cases, you don't need to fully understand, relate to, or agree with another person's story to want to help alleviate their suffering. It merely takes a desire to help and the will to share your heart.

Sympathy

So how does sympathy factor in?

> **Sympathy:** Sympathy is a feeling of sincere concern for someone who is experiencing something difficult or painful.[5]

Sympathy is feeling compassion, sorrow, or pity *for* the other person's suffering. Empathy is feeling *with* another.

People who are deeply grieving need your empathy more than your sympathy.

CHAPTER 2

What To Do

YOU MAY BE FEELING AWKWARD or unsure about how to help, but keep in mind, your loved one is probably feeling awkward about receiving help or even knowing what they need.

If you're unsure, just be candid. Simply say, "I don't know what to say or do to help you right now, but I want you to know I care. I am here with you." That alone can be a great comfort and a nice start.

There are many ways you can be a source of reassurance. This was explored in my last book on how to comfort someone who has lost their mother, and it's worth detailing and elaborating on further here.

These are the things we need after our first parent dies and still need when we lose our second.

To simplify, what you can do can be broken down into three categories:

- Practical Assistance
- Physical Comfort
- Emotional Support

Practical Assistance

The early days of grief are the hardest. The bereaved person is usually in a state of shock and denial—even when the death is expected.

Very often, they are too emotionally exhausted and physically drained to deal with everyday tasks. Yet life does move forward.

Saying something like, "Please tell me if I can help with anything," puts the burden on the grieving. The truth is, they may not even know what they need, how to ask, or feel uncomfortable accepting help.

The most generous thing you can do is offer specific assistance. Offer practical assistance, including:

- Grocery shopping. (Stocking up on the food basics and also practical items like toilet paper, soap, eggs, milk, coffee, etc.)
- Cooking at their house if they'd like company, or bringing over precooked meals that are easy to serve. (Bring extra in small batches for easy defrosting and heating.)
- Housework or hiring a maid service to come over and clean for the day.
- Doing the laundry or dropping clothes off at the dry cleaner.
- Running errands. (This is a huge energy saver.)
- Mowing their lawn, watering their plants.
- Taking out their trash bins and bringing them back in the next day. (Simple chores can be the most tedious and draining.)
- Walking the dog (or bathing a pet) if needed.

- Taking on responsibilities like picking the kids up from school or taking them to and from play dates, the movies, or special excursions.

OTHER THOUGHTFUL SUGGESTIONS:

- Give them a gift card for their favorite restaurant. This gives them a choice of convenient delivery from a place they love or allows them a treat if they'd like to get out of the house.
- Bring a case of water. Remind them, lovingly, to stay hydrated.
- Bring a box of thank-you notes and stamps for post-service correspondence.
- Offer to take their car for a wash or fill it up with gas.
- Bring over paper plates, cups, utensils, and napkins so they don't have to do dishes.
- Buy them extra handkerchiefs or boxed/packet tissues if they tend to release tears. They will come in handy in the months ahead, especially at memorials.
- Make your loved one a self-care basket for the pampering they need. Include things like lavender Epsom salt bubble bath, aromatherapy candles, and spa music.
- If they don't already have one, get them a breakfast in bed tray to make sure they eat and feel cared for, whether they can get out of bed or not.

PHYSICAL COMFORT

It's a very strange thing, grief. The one grieving often wants to be alone but not lonely.

If you live with someone who just lost their last surviving parent, try making open communication a priority. Does your loved one need physical comfort or space?

You might think a hug is the best thing you can offer a loved one or friend in pain. That's not necessarily true when it comes to grief.

Many people need physical touch and comfort. Others may not want physical contact of any kind or pull back out of fear that they're already on the constant verge of crying, and a hug could break the dam of tears.

Try not to take things personally. When in doubt, just open your arms and invite a hug if it will help. If not, let them know that squeeze is there on standby when they are ready.

If you don't live with the bereaved, see if they'd like you to come over. Would they like a home-cooked meal? Go out and see a movie? Go for a walk together and get some air? Maybe just plop on the couch and watch TV?

Let them know you're available to bring popcorn and the gift of silent company.

If all they want is to be alone, don't be offended. Just say something like, "Of course. Rest. Take care of you right now."

The best thing you can do is give them space until they're ready to accept more.

Emotional Support

While there's nothing you can do to take away your friend's or loved one's pain, there are numerous ways to provide the kind of emotional support that can help them on their healing journey. To show you care, remember to:

- Give your full attention. Put your phone away, not just face-down. Stash it out of sight to show your focus is on them.
- Open your heart.
- Dare to be vulnerable. It gives them permission to do the same.
- Be an active listener. Be attentive; listen to understand, not respond. Reflect on what's being said and remember this information for later.
- Encourage the one grieving to talk, cry, ramble if they need to. This is the healthiest way they can begin to process their grief.
- Acknowledge their pain.
- Validate their feelings.
- Don't interrupt. When they share, let them speak freely. They need to flow with whatever train of thought or feeling they have.
- If they can't find a word, be patient. Brain fog is very common. Stepping in can stop their mental processing and be misinterpreted as hurrying them along.
- Tell them often: "Take your time."
- Let them know it's okay to fall apart and that they are safe with you.
- Don't put expectations or demands on them.

- Know their parents' names. Use those names, when appropriate.
- Ask questions about their parents. Get to know more about who they were. It is often a comfort for people who are grieving to talk about their mother and/or father.
- Ask about favorite childhood meals and comfort foods. Remember to bring them in the future.
- Let the person who is grieving repeat the same story if they need to. Don't edit them. This is very helpful in releasing emotions associated with their trauma and grief.
- Offer extra support on special days, including holidays, their parents' birthdays, and dates when a parent died, which often reawakens grief. Be particularly sensitive on these occasions.
- Be flexible. If your friend or loved one goes through mood swings, needs to change plans at the last minute, or have problems committing, it's usually not that they're flakey; they're just trying to manage the unpredictable emotional waves.
- Ask them how they are *today*, not the generic, "How are you?" This acknowledges that you recognize that it's a hard time overall and they are hurting. Ask how they are at this moment.
- Be consistent.
- Be there for the emotional long haul. Check in and send cards or texts in the months ahead. Grieving goes on long after the funeral is over and the cards and flowers have stopped. Be the exception if you can.

Emotional support needs to begin as soon as you hear news of the death. The first hours and days are the hardest for the bereaved. Reach out by way of phone call, text, send flowers, a handwritten card, or a comfort basket.

Offer to attend the service or memorial if they'd like that extra support. Attending a service is not only a sign of caring but also a sign of respect for your friend's parent and a chance to get to know them better through the stories told and people who attend.

CHAPTER 3

What Not to Do

Now THAT YOU HAVE A better idea of what to do for a loved one in grief, let's go over some of the things you should not do. When in doubt, let these words from the Dalai Lama guide you: "Our prime purpose in life is to help others. And if you can't help them, at least don't hurt them."[6]

Grieving is a very delicate time, which is why the grief ally also needs to be sensitive.

Here are a few things to avoid in your effort to help:

- Don't judge. Everyone's process is different.
- Don't offer unsolicited advice. This is their journey.
- Don't rush them to "get over it." No one enjoys the pain of grief, and it's not something they can just snap out of. Any timeline pressure is a false expectation. That would say more about your impatience than their effort to heal.
- Don't try to control the conversation.
- Never point out the fact that they may be themself right now. They are not. Grief changes a person as they work through their pain.

- Don't make assumptions based on outward appearances. The bereaved person may look fine on the outside, while they're suffering inside.
- If you have different religious or spiritual views, don't impose your values on them.
- Try not to hold temporary outbursts against them. Their nervous system is not regulated while heavily grieving.
- Don't dry their tears, as that stops the flow of emotions associated with them. You can slide a tissue box to them but let them cry so they can let it out. It's a great release.
- Don't try to lighten the mood. The one grieving needs to feel whatever they need to feel.
- Don't abandon them—emotionally or physically—at a time when they are already feeling at their most vulnerable and alone.
- Feelings and needs will change frequently. Don't assume "no thank you" one day means "no thank you" for the duration.

CHAPTER 4

What to Say

Providing comfort isn't about finding the "perfect" words; there aren't any when it comes to grief. It's all about offering solace and presence during a time of loss.

If you can't find the words yourself, these suggestions may help:

- "I wish I had the right words to say; just know I care about you, and I am here for you."
- "I can't begin to imagine the scope of everything you're going through. I hope you know how much I care about you."
- "Whenever you want to talk, no matter what time it is, I'm only a phone call away."
- "I'm thinking of you, with love."
- "I can't take your pain away, but I can always give hugs when you need one."
- "Even if you just want to sit in silence, we can do that."
- "Anything you need, I will do for you. Lean on me. I am always here for you."
- "I love you."

CHAPTER 5

What Not to Say

WE ALL GROW UP AWARE of a bucket of cliché responses we assume will help someone who is dealing with loss. The following have good intentions behind them, but they can sting:

- **"I'm sorry for your loss."** This is undoubtedly the most overused phrase of all. The bereaved didn't lose something inconsequential like their keys. They just endured the monumental death of a parent. It's better to personalize the phrase with the parent's name, i.e., "I am so sorry for the loss of your beloved mother, Lynn."
- **"I know exactly how you feel."** No, you don't. Every love is different. Every loss is different. No one can ever truly understand how another person feels in their grief.
- **"At least…"** Don't ever start a sentence with those two words in this situation. This *minimizes* the loss. Your intention may be to cheer them up, but this isn't the way. Acknowledging their pain will.
- **"They're in a better place."** Don't do it. And do you mean *"Better than here with me?"* This phrase often hurts the person in pain, whether they believe in an afterlife or not.

- **"You're just..."** Another bad opener that minimizes and invalidates the feelings of the grieving.
- **"You should."** Should is a shame word. Also, it's a good time to resist the temptation to tell someone who is suffering what to do and how to do it.
- **"You're so strong!"** This gives an expectation that they should be strong, when in reality, they may not be showing how truly broken or weak they may feel on the inside. The bereaved may be "putting on a brave face" and not tapping into something they may not have access to at the moment.
- **"I'm worried about you."** This one puts the focus on *your* feelings and pressure on them to behave differently for your sake. Not helpful.
- **"Your mother/father wouldn't want to see you so sad."** Never appropriate. Especially if you didn't know the person's parents.
- **"Everything happens for a reason."** There is never a good reason to lose someone you love. This phrase is hollow and hurtful.
- **"Look at all you have to be thankful for."** Even if a person has much to be grateful for, right now that's not important. The person who died is.
- **"Now you can focus on your own life again."** Even if caring for parents was time-consuming, there's no joy in this kind of freedom.
- **"He/She/They lived a long life."** It's not about the years you had with someone; it's about the years you won't have with them going forward.
- **"You will see them again."** This tends to be less than comforting in the present moment. People grieving a

person who died want them now. Still. And not everyone shares the same beliefs about life and death or an afterlife.
- **"Time heals all wounds."** Death is far deeper than any wound. The pain of losing someone may indeed lessen over time but never goes away completely. This is whitewashing the profound loss the person grieving is feeling *at this moment.*

CHAPTER 6

You Can't Pour from an Empty Cup

BEING AN EMOTIONAL SUPPORT PERSON isn't always easy.

No matter how much you want to care for someone, you can't wear yourself down trying to help them. Allowing yourself to get to the point where you are physically, emotionally, and mentally exhausted helps no one, including yourself.

The key is to go into self-care mode long before you slide into burnout. It's a daily practice that you give to yourself, and that ultimately benefits others.

The metaphor, "You can't pour from an empty cup," is true. It's a valuable reminder that you cannot give to others without first taking care of yourself.

COMPASSION FATIGUE

Without balance, caring for others can lead to a type of burnout known as <u>compassion fatigue</u>.

It can leave people feeling depleted and unable to muster concern for others. This emotional and physical exhaustion can lead to diminished feelings of empathy, increased irritability, resentment, and apathy.

When this happens, the drive that once fueled your desire to help can crash.

"To try to prevent this, be mindful of how you are feeling. If you notice you are struggling to access your empathy and compassion, or it feels like it's too much for you, take a step back. Remember that your mental health is also important and that you can't help others if you don't take care of yourself,"[7] says Kendra Cherry, MSEd, a psychosocial rehabilitation specialist and author of the *Everything Psychology Book*.

CHAPTER 7

The Blessing of a Companion in Grief

IF YOU'RE MOVED TO HELP someone who has just suffered the death of a parent, be a companion in grief, regardless of how well you know the person. Even a little touch—by way of a supportive call, text, or email—can have a lasting impact.

I've heard countless stories from people in grief who were disappointed by those they thought would be there for them, who, for whatever reason, just disappeared. The most common and mistaken assumption is that the person grieving must already have a close circle of friends around them.

Way too many people, including me at times, were left very much alone on the island of grief.

But there are also many stories of both friends and remarkable people outside the expected circle of friends and family who showed up without hesitation or expectation.

I remember turning around at my mother's memorial service, surprised to see a friend from work sitting by herself in the back of the chapel. She just smiled at me and nodded. That small gesture was big. It not only made me feel supported during that gut-wrenching time, but it was a beautiful show of respect for my mother, whom she had never met, and brought additional emotional support for me as a friend.

The ones who show up through thick and thin are true blessings. They seem to be the ones who know what you need, even when you don't.

A dear friend I rarely get to see lives out of state, but I still felt her right there with me after my father died. She left a simple, loving phone message offering soft comfort—not just honoring my dad's death but was also the first to acknowledge how hard it was to lose *both* parents.

She knows because she's been there. That's empathy in action.

I was touched when a childhood friend of mine sent a very personal, handwritten card after my father died that I'll save forever. She shared funny and sweet memories of my dad and how much a part of our youth he was, as well as acknowledging and validating feelings I was experiencing since his death.

Another friend brought some groceries to my doorstep that included some of my favorite childhood meals and treats just to make sure I'd eat. She didn't give me a chance to say "No," which I would have.

A brief encounter with a complete stranger also brought comfort. I had overloaded a flatbed trolley with plants at the local nursery for my dad's honor garden after he died. I could barely see over it, and much less maneuver it.

An older woman just stood and watched, amused by the sight of my ambitious determination. She offered to help and cheerfully admired the choice of flowers and plants.

When I told her what I had planned for them all, her face changed, and she told me she had just lost her dad a few years prior, and that the following day was his birthday.

I could see it in her eyes. "It's still fresh," I said.

"Yeah," she answered with a slow nod.

We chattered for a while. I asked her about her father, what his name is, and we each found some relief, heart-to-heart comfort, and understanding in the company of another stranger. Both of us walked away smiling.

Companions in grief are all around us.

I'm amazed by friends who become distant and strangers who become close in the face of loss.

Presence is an energy of love that can be felt, even when you can't physically be by your friend or loved one's side.

More than nurtured, I felt seen in those moments. Even better, I felt my parents were seen too. That was a bonus I could not have expected.

Trust is earned in the smallest gestures of authentic care and connection.

Our companions in grief leave an impression on our hearts. The memory of their compassion often buoys us through hard times with kindness we won't soon forget.

PART IV: PURPOSE & THE PATH FORWARD

"Just when the caterpillar thought the world was over, it became a butterfly."

— CHUANG TZU

CHAPTER 1

The Arc of Life

*"New beginnings are often disguised
as painful endings."*

— Lao Tzu

Life in Stages

Life happens in stages. First infancy, then the carefree innocence of childhood, to adulthood and midlife, to our golden years, and ultimately—inevitably—our own passing.

The arc of life is built into our stay here on Earth. Change, the one true constant in life, is an unavoidable, integral part of our human experience. Naturally, apprehension over the unknown is an expected response when we are confronted with so many new things beyond our control.

I had to come to terms with a couple of life's non-negotiables when I lost my parents. First and foremost, among those lessons is: We don't make the rules. We do, however, have the ability to choose how we react in the toughest moments.

We can fight the tide, or we can go with the flow.

Personally, I had to allow myself to sit with "the uncomfortable" for a while—to get comfortable with the uncomfortable. I had to surrender to the fact that with each change comes some level of grief as we mourn who and what we are leaving behind while also getting real about the known and unknown that lies ahead.

In the gap between the old lives we have lost and the new ones we have yet to create, it isn't easy to sit with the swirling tide of emotions—to feel them rise and fall and then come crashing back again.

But that's how we process grief.

During this pause, try to remember it's a temporary stay on the path forward. It's not the end of the road.

I think part of coping well with bereavement depends upon how we frame it. I don't think of it as "this part of my life is over." That just feels too sad.

Instead, I accept this stage in life is now "complete."

This juncture in life begins a new you and a new form of connection with your parents in spirit.

With practice, you can go with the natural current of life.

Will you choose to sink or swim?

I Don't Feel Like Me

After the death of both parents, many say, as I did: "I don't feel like myself anymore."

That's because you're not the "you" you used to know. The person had physically present parents, and it takes time to get to know this new version of yourself.

It is very common for this inward-looking phase to plunge us into the "dark night of the soul," where meaning in life seems out of reach and little makes sense anymore.

A dark night of the soul is a process where we face who and what we thought we were, and let those thoughts and beliefs go. This period helps us shed old skin and an old identity to reveal what is underneath. It serves to transform us into more of the essence of our true being.

Besides deep sadness, this can lead to promise in the freshness of this transformational moment. You can rewrite your story; change the rules. Live life on your terms. It takes a while to get there, of course.

Show yourself compassion and patience. It's a process to detach from the old identity and transition into a new one.

I had to revisit so much of what I learned after the death of my mother and put it into practice again after the death of my father. So much was familiar territory, but so much was far more profound and all-new after they both died.

It's challenging to realize we are not the same as we once were and never will be. But there is such validation in recognizing that fact. We're not superhuman; we're simply human. We love, and we hurt. It's perfectly natural to feel the way we do.

Permission to feel broken or blue is the gift we give ourselves as we move toward healing.

A big part of moving forward is releasing expectations—the mental picture—of who we were, where we thought our life was going, and who we thought we would be.

Denying reality brings pain and suffering. Release yourself from its grasp.

This is your chrysalis moment, like the metamorphosis from caterpillar to butterfly.

For now, rest. When you are ready, you'll have wings to fly.

Remember you've survived every transition through life to date, and although this one is probably the most complicated and painful, you can do it again.

You *will* do it again.

THE FEAR OF DYING

After our parents die, our own mortality becomes palpable. It is a universal fear that usually begins haunting us in childhood, but now, we can no longer hide from this inevitable reality.

For many adult orphans I've spoken to, the passing of their first parent brought death closer and made it more real. But if it involved the parent they were closest to, there was often less fear. In those situations, many said they actually looked forward to the day they'd be reunited with their mother or father.

By the time of the second parent's death, not only is mortality undeniable, but it also brings up the fear of *how* we will die.

How do we move forward and lessen the fear of dying and of the unknown? It's kind of a big obstacle in the road in front of us.

I went to a source I thought might know—and who's always there for me—Alexa (Amazon's cloud-based voice service). I once asked "her" jokingly, "Alexa, do I look fat?" She answered, "I think you're perfect just the way you are." (Awww. That one always knows just what to say.)

So, I inquired, "Alexa, how do I overcome fear of the unknown or a fear of dying?" She offered the *best* advice: "One of the best ways to overcome your fear of the unknown is to learn from others who have been in your shoes." She also suggested focusing on the things in life we *can* control.

That's it! So simple. There is no cure for these fears, but there are ways to learn to cope and, hopefully, lessen your anxiety.

Vocalizing fears and listening to others share their apprehensions can reduce the sense of isolation. Of all the issues we confront as adult orphans, our own mortality is among the hardest to come to terms with.

Learning from spiritual and religious teachers and other professionals provided additional guidance.

In a lecture on her book, *Embracing the Unknown: Life Lessons from the Tibetan Book of the Dead*,[1] Pema Chödrön talked about life, death, change, and "welcoming the unwelcome" as we navigate the impermanent nature of life.

A wise Buddhist teacher of hers suggested she not think of endings as "letting go." That seems like a heavy lift. Instead, he suggested using the phrase "letting be."

That creates a more effortless approach during the inevitable end stages of all things.

We usually look at birth and death in terms of a life span, which can take place over decades. But Chödrön points out that every day, we go through continual cycles of birth and death.

There is impermanence within each and every day. As we get familiar with the process, the notion is we grow accustomed to the cycles of life, become less resistant, and develop an appreciation for the in-between moments that make up a lifetime.

"Death isn't just something that happens at the end," says Chödrön. "Life is continually arising, dwelling, ceasing, and arising. It's a cycle that goes on every day and continues to go on forever."

She explains that everything is temporary, shifting, and changing all the time in life: the seasons, the shadow of sunlight as it moves across the earth from sunrise to sunset, a lunch with a friend, the moon above as it waxes and wanes, etc. These are all moments with a beginning, a middle, and an end.

To get comfortable with the natural flow of change, she suggests making it a practice to note the small beginning and ending cycles of each day. That can help in accepting the beginning and ending cycles in life and in accepting "how everything is impermanent, shifting, and changing all the time."

To overcome our fear of death, she says, "I think overcoming our discomfort with impermanence is a good starting place." This, I found, was an enlightening new way to look at mortality.

"When we resist change, it's called suffering," she says, suggesting we get playful with impermanence and let it be part of life that we actually notice.

By making a practice of noting the continuous cycles of birth and death throughout your day, you will begin to get a feeling of the flow of impermanence. You'll directly experience how nothing exists in a fixed way.

Chödrön wrote that as we become more accustomed to this flow, we start seeing things in fresh ways. "I have also recommended this to many people, and the feedback I've received suggests that many who do this practice will eventually lose their fear of death. It makes death become so familiar that it stops feeling threatening."

When I find myself in a fearful or resistant state, I look at the words "Let it be" tattooed on my wrist and repeat: "This is about 'letting be' not 'letting go.'"

You can apply your own reminder to shift your thinking if you find yourself slipping. Perhaps twirl a ring on your finger, lightly snap a bracelet, or tap your wristwatch. Use this as a reset tool to reset your mind, instead of heading down a negative path. Remember the value of positive neuroplasticity. You hold the power to rewire your brain in ways that bring comfort, not fear.

I found this is a much softer way to think about the natural process of growing older, about uncertainties and insecurities that may pop up, and all the life events we tend to struggle with.

I hope it helps you too.

LONELINESS

Along with the fear of death and questions about our identity, a deep sense of loneliness sets in for most of us as "life goes on" in the world outside, while inside, our world has stopped. This is the great disconnect that can leave many feeling in no-man's-land between two worlds.

Grief is incredibly lonely. Pulling out of it can feel impossible sometimes.

First, we physically lose people we love to death, then, oftentimes, we lose family members and friends in the process. The losses that accumulate are painful and difficult. Having just the company of our thoughts can lead to a sense of profound isolation.

Chödrön also addressed this topic in another insightful book, *When Things Fall Apart: Heart Advice for Difficult Times*,[2] where she suggests we try to see emptiness as an experience to cultivate rather than avoid and use this (temporary) experience to learn and grow from.

When life as you know it ends—and loneliness is too much to bear—there is a tendency to either block or avoid the experience by getting any kind of ground under our feet. We may reach for whatever may comfort us by way of food, drugs or alcohol, social media scrolling, shopping, or other familiar distractions.

That is an effort to solve the problem of isolation from the outside in.

Loneliness, she writes, is not a problem to be solved. Instead, she suggests we take this time to figure out our emotions, sit in the emptiness, and let emotions wash over us. "Letting be" any emotions as they are.

Rather than trying to fill the void, Chödrön suggests treating it as a discipline where, instead of turning away, we gently come into the present moment and become willing to sit still. Unanchored. Alone.

This taps into our core sensitivity associated with loss, but then also heals it.

Sit just long enough to acknowledge, "This is just the way things really are."

For now.

It's natural to want to run away from feelings of isolation. But, especially in a time of uncertainty, coming back and relaxing into something as familiar as loneliness is "good discipline for realizing the profundity of the unresolved moments of our lives," Chödrön says, adding, "We are cheating ourselves when we run away from the ambiguity of loneliness."

This kind of separation, she continues, allows us to look honestly at our own minds. We can learn to drop our ideas of who we think we ought to be or who we think other people think we should be. "We give up and just look directly with compassion and humor at who we are. Then, loneliness is no threat and heartache, no punishment." This alone time doesn't provide any immediate resolution; it challenges us to step into a world of honest introspection. "This is called 'the sacred path of the warrior.'"

Chödrön suggests if you wake up feeling alone, try to use it as an opportunity to go within. Nothing horribly wrong is happening. "In the moment of sadness and longing, relax and touch the limitless space of the human heart."

In time, we grow through these periods of loneliness as the healing warriors we are.

THE THICK OF IT

"I sat with my anger long enough until she told me her real name was grief."

— C.S. LEWIS

When my mom died, I felt a part of me died too. I struggled afterward to find "me," my purpose, and my identity again.

For anyone who feels like giving up, please know there was a time I did too.

Rough days may follow, but the balance between good days and bad will even out in time and soon tip in favor of healing.

I didn't believe it when I was in the thick of it, but it's true.

Even after my dad died, every time I felt that punch of sadness in my gut, I had to remind myself, with my hand over my heart and gentle pats on my chest, to: "Hold tight. This feeling will pass."

Forgiveness & Moving Forward

It takes time to fully absorb the impact of a major loss.

When my mom died first, I didn't know how I'd ever survive. As I grew stronger again, I still worried that the grief inside was the last thread that still connected us. It showed that she lived; that she mattered.

It reflected my love for her. My fear, back then, was that if I let go of my grief, I'd be letting go of her. And I didn't want to lose her all over again.

Her life mattered. I didn't want "healing" to ever mean I would "move on" and forget her.

That's a common fear among so many of us. But the truth is, as you grow through grief, you take the love with you. The parent-and-child energy bond continues. Forever.

That's one promise that life guarantees us.

Having experienced loss once, I had some confidence I could work through my grief after my dad's death, and I did. I am. It's all an ongoing, lifelong process.

It has been comforting to listen to others share their stories. It reminds me we can't rush things, and grief isn't something we can ever wrap up in a tidy bow and be done with. That expectation is a recipe for disappointment.

A longtime friend, Jim, reflected and told me, "Speaking from my own experience, it can be a very long process. Almost 30 years after losing my mom and 10 years after my dad, I am still working things through."

I have been able to process a lot of conflicted emotions through talking with others, journaling, and releasing through dreams. While my mom was always my most solid source of love and my biggest cheerleader, my dad, who grew up in a very strict household where love wasn't displayed, was unintentionally my greatest source of hurt.

Of course, each sibling will have a different relationship with their parents and will grieve differently as a result, but this was *my* personal experience that needed healing.

From my perspective, my dad had wonderful qualities, including his intelligence, solid work ethic, dry wit, and willingness to share his joy of fishing, camping, and the outdoors with his daughters. He would show love in his own way by bringing miniature dolls back for us after business trips abroad, making cinnamon rolls and scrambled eggs on weekends, playing sports with us, and coaching our youth softball team.

As my sisters and I grew older, especially after our mom died, he would always have flowers for us when we visited him at his house. He tried to be better. To show we were valued.

He was a decent man. A good man. He did love, in his way. He was also a product of the times and the large Irish immigrant family he grew up in.

My dad could be emotionally unavailable, judgmental, and tough—especially with me. In his final years, I asked him why he had been so hard on me my whole life. I worked endlessly for his approval which was next to impossible to get, even when I achieved some great successes.

He told me, "Because I felt it would make you stronger."

Stronger? I told him, no, that it actually left me with no self-esteem, never feeling good enough, and on a never-ending chase for validation through success and people-pleasing. I am grateful we had long talks in the end, however, and that I got to understand him better.

In his eyes, he really thought he was making me a better person. He didn't understand that it wasn't the way to parent a sensitive, already resourceful child.

After 50+ years together, the old him began to soften. With tears in his eyes, he told me he loved me. He also finally said he was proud of my achievements, and that I should be too.

In his final years, all inroads in our father/daughter healing were lost to his disease. And I had to let go of some hurtful things he did and said at the end and remember who he was at his spiritual core.

There is love there, and he did the best he could.

I may have grown up feeling emotionally abandoned, but I realized that if I didn't release the pain of the past, it would be my own happiness now I'd be abandoning, and *that was in my power to control.*

My healing was on me. My responsibility.

I chose to forgive him—and myself—for not learning this lesson sooner.

I talked about this with a friend I've known since childhood who's very soulful and wise. She knew my dad. She also lost both parents and twisted herself into a human pretzel to get approval from her father that never came. She said, "How odd is it to look back and see all the damage done, and for what? Now they are gone, and there is nothing more to prove or change."

At first, I was apprehensive about sharing the not-so-pretty part of my father/daughter relationship, as well as my own insecurities, and I didn't want to tarnish his image in death. But I'm glad I shared. We both benefited from a deep, authentic talk.

After sharing my conflicted feelings—and voicing guilt about feeling them—I told her, "I hope my sad is okay." I didn't want to emotionally dump. She replied, "Your sad was earned, damn it. That hurts my soul. This is complex stuff. It's not all roses."

There it was. With a little validation and a giant exhale, I felt lighter by dropping some of the weight of resentment. I was ready to move forward. It was time.

Having gone through it once, you'll also come to see that, just like grief, healing is not linear. You may climb one emotional mountain, just to slip down sometimes, again and again.

But time gives you the resilience to get back up a little faster and a little stronger with each setback. Dormant issues may pop up, and that's common, but you'll have the tools to address them.

It's true what they say, grief comes in waves, but in between those waves is where we learn to catch our breath and breathe deeply again.

The in-between is where healing begins and where your power lies.

When you catch your proverbial breath and are ready for your next step, remember… you will not move on, you will simply move forward.

Signs You Are Healing

"And suddenly you know: It's time to start something new and trust the magic of beginnings."
— Meister Eckhart

When you've already lost one parent, you're probably well aware that grief never completely ends. It comes in cycles, not stages.

In time, it gets smaller in intensity. As we grow around it, we move into a place where grief no longer casts its long shadow over every area of our life.

Healing isn't a destination; it means grief no longer controls us and we are continuing to move forward. It means we are ready for some semblance of our life back. We're more resilient now.

The huge, ragged rock of grief we carried in our pocket becomes a polished memory stone that still connects us to our parents. As we heal, we begin to feel that the load is lighter and can find comfort in carrying this artifact of love with us.

With time, you will wake up without heartache and sadness as the first thing on your mind. Your body will be more regulated and relaxed, and hope will begin to float to the surface again.

Your safe cocoon begins to crack open.

Your desire to live and engage with life comes back online—ever so slightly at first, then with more gusto.

When the weight of all you carry—the sadness, resentment, guilt, loneliness, fear—begins to subside, you create more space to allow more of life back in.

More happy memories will find their way in and replace the sad ones. You'll find yourself smiling more than crying. The brain fog starts to lift, and you won't just go with the flow more easily... *you will become the flow.*

You will be motivated to make a positive change for the future without the pain of the past.

That's when you'll know you are healing and on your path forward.

CHAPTER 2

The Hero's Journey

"Everything is possible for the one who believes."

— MARK 9:23

I ALWAYS THOUGHT THE PROCESS of grief was similar to the hero's journey—also known as the monomyth—that common narrative pattern found in stories throughout time and cultures, where the archetypical hero is reluctantly called to action, is victorious in a crisis, and comes home transformed.

This universal structure was first recognized in one of my favorite books, *The Hero with a Thousand Faces*[1] by author and mythologist Joseph Campbell. In the 1949 book, he outlined the hero's journey in three basic stages that were often found in myths, movies, and literature across many cultures, from Homer's *The Odyssey* to *Star Wars* to *Finding Nemo*.

The framework, basically, can be broken down into three stages: the hero is summoned to a call or adventure, often resisting before embarking on his journey; then he faces a series of trials and personal challenges, where he is often assisted by allies;

finally, leading to a return home where he is transformed for the better with new wisdom and insights.

This framework also mirrors the path of the journey through grief.

In grief, a loved one's death is the call or challenge. That propels us through the threshold of the grieving process and our inner journey to understand our emotions, adjust to life without our loved ones, and find ways to heal. We gain insight, growth, and personal evolution through this experience. Finally, our winding path leads us back home transformed.

Rather than looking at ourselves as victims of a painful event, I felt it was more empowering to consider ourselves the heroes of our own story as we move toward growth, restoration, and healing.

The protagonists of those classic tales all emerge triumphant through their strength, resilience, and ability to adapt and grow as they learn more about themselves.

The monomyth's stages can serve as inspiration, maybe even guidance, as we make our way through our own personal hero's journey and back to ourselves.

Make Change Your Friend

Finding joy in life again can often feel elusive while we're deep in grief. I questioned how to go about finding it again myself.

I really enjoy *The Mel Robbins Podcast*. Robbins is a witty, sharp, and relatable New York Times best-selling author, motivational coach, and expert on personal transformation.

One of her podcasts opened with how she and her husband decided to have a spontaneous campout in their Vermont backyard under the stars. The next morning, she reflected on how much fun that was and why they didn't do more things like that.

"How did I let life get so boring?" she pondered.

Then it dawned on her, "Mel, maybe life isn't boring. Maybe *you* got boring." That happens when we get a little too comfortable in our daily routine.

In her episode, "How to Make Your Life Exciting Again"[2] with Dr. Tali Sharot, a neuroscientist from MIT and University College, London, they discuss proven ways, based on brain science, to shake up your life and rediscover joy again.

Harris noted how so many of us fear change, but Dr. Sharot actually uncovered a link between change and experiencing happiness and joy in life.

Our ability to change, to push ourselves to experience and learn new things in our life is foundational to us enjoying our life and having moments of joy, according to her guest.

They discussed when we fall into a daily routine that doesn't challenge our brain, which can lead us to feel habitually stuck, unmotivated, uninspired, and reacting less to old familiar stimuli that once brought pleasure.

The brain needs the "new" to get neurons fired up.

Firsts of any kind can be new and stimulating. That's when they tend to elicit the most excitement. That can alter our mood, so a continuing effort to learn something new, change things up, and look at life through new eyes is key to joy.

Think about when you feel the happiest and carefree in your life. Many say it was during childhood—when we did not get stuck in routines—but we were constantly playing, growing, learning, having fun, socializing, and trying new adventures.

Our brain was charged and challenged almost daily.

Sharot's research shows the direct connection between how much happiness you feel and the amount that you are willing to change.

The quick happiness hack, she says, introduces variety into your life. Learn more. If you change your environment or habits, it will change your brain processes, which also enhances creativity.

To shake things up, Sharot suggests trying one new action; it could lead to a big difference in your life. "Think about something you want to learn, think about a new skill that you want to have, maybe somewhere you want to visit, try a new dish to make."

Research shows novelty will boost your happiness while also inspiring you to get into the habit of trying new things.

Ask yourself, "What do I look forward to?" "What do I enjoy?" Find your joy and make a plan.

Arrange things you can look forward to because even the anticipation of something new and fun will trigger your brain toward happiness. "Just being proactive about putting things on your calendar in the future to look forward to is a way to hack happiness in your life now," said Robbins.

Sharot suggests you "experiment in living." Try new things. Change things up. Take things out of your life or try them in a new way if they aren't promoting the happiness and joy you seek.

Harris says creating a better life is possible. "It is so amazing how small changes are vital for your happiness." If you want a different tomorrow, make a small change today.

When the search for "new" is on, this simple proposition can serve as a compass for you along the journey toward joy, where change is used for your good.

Purpose

Besides healthy change, a sense of purpose also helps move us along on our journey. It can give us a reason to get up in the morning, a reason for living, guide our decisions, shape our goals, and determine how we show up in the world.

Purpose brings light and meaning to our lives.

A devastating loss is often a turning point where our basic sense of direction is among the many casualties felt. It often leaves us wandering aimlessly for some time. The things we used to enjoy can, and often do, lose their appeal.

Our motivation for life can suddenly evaporate, and creating our new normal becomes challenging.

In *Man's Search for Meaning*, the best-selling classic now considered to be one of the most influential books of the 20th century, Viktor Frankl writes, "The primary motivation for living is to find meaning. The goal is to figure out how to live in such a way that gives purpose and meaning to existence."[3]

Frankl, a Nazi concentration camp survivor, found purpose in the most horrific of circumstances, leaving a legacy that has the ability to inspire anyone and everyone to find a deeper, richer value in their lives, no matter what their situation.

Our power, he suggests, lies in the fact that we have the freedom to choose to transcend disappointments and suffering in life by finding meaning in every moment. While loss can leave us devastated, it can also be a catalyst for change that involves a mini life audit—a time to set new priorities and goals and take stock of what really matters to us.

Many who are going through the early stages of this reorienting period are no longer certain about their outer purpose in life. What drove them before often no longer does. "What am I doing with my life?" is a thought that often arises, along with a little soul-searching into what truly inspires us.

Some suggest creating new purpose and meaning despite our grief involves aligning our outer purpose (career, relationships, family, etc.) with our inner purpose (what brings us joy, fulfillment, etc.)

"It is precisely through the onset of old age, through loss or personal tragedy, that the spiritual dimension would traditionally come into people's lives. This is to say, their inner purpose would emerge only as their outer purpose collapsed and the shell of the ego would begin to crack open," writes Eckhart Tolle in *A New Earth: Awakening Your Life's Purpose*.[4]

"Outer purpose alone is always relative, unstable, impermanent. This does not mean that you should not be engaged in those activities. It means you should connect them to your inner primary purpose, so that a deeper meaning flows into what you do," says Tolle.

According to his teachings, if we can merge renewed inner and outer purpose, it can allow us to live a more authentic life, which leads to more joyfulness. "This is enormously empowering," he says.

As you move through grief, reviving a sense of purpose can begin slowly with a simple to-do list for the day. Just getting out of bed, brushing your teeth, eating breakfast, feeding your pets, or walking the dog can bring meaning to your day. We begin with small steps, crossing little accomplishments off our daily list and considering that a win.

With time, your renewed drive can include integrating your grief with ways that honor the memory of your loved one. You can show their life continues to have importance and that the spiritual connection you share is still alive.

Purpose can also include engaging in activities you enjoyed together, becoming involved in charitable endeavors connected to them, or simply walking through life in a way that lets you shine the best of them through you.

Allow yourself time to experiment with what reignites your pilot light. It can be anything. A sense of purpose can be as simple as learning a new hobby or sport. Give yourself something to look forward to and be open to that spark of life again.

Research suggests that people who do are more likely to be happier, more resilient, and more successful with more satisfaction in their lives.

Live life with purpose... on purpose.

Purpose and meaning are closely tied. Purpose gives life direction; meaning gives life value.

After walking through her own journey through grief, Lisa M. Shulman, MD, author of *Before and After Loss*,[5] shared some of her own personal reflections on navigating through loss and finding her way again. "At times," she says, "I'm caught up in self-doubts, but more often, I believe inner work will transform to direction and purpose."

It's another process to naturally go with. "I sense this can't be forced but needs to gestate organically. I acknowledge future possibilities but continue to be realistic about what's been lost: the innocence, the shelter, the joy of the *before life...* both a loss and a legacy to build on."

Like an alchemist, I found writing two self-help grief recovery guidebooks—and establishing a companion bereavement support group for each—was what helped me turn pain into purpose. I think once we've had the privilege of being helped by others through times of grief, like I had, we owe it to those going through similar experiences to reach back and offer the same support.

It helped give me a reason to show up for myself and for others. And it was also a way to honor my mother and father.

Meaning-Making

In the aftershock of loss, when life feels so dimmed, there is a deep need to make sense of it all. In those moments, it helps to allow yourself space for personal reflection on what can be learned from the grief experience.

Meaning-making can support restructuring your life in a way that helps honor those you love rather than feeling like you have lost them forever. We may lose their body to death, but never their memory.

Dr. Robert A. Neimeyer is a world-renowned grief expert and professor of psychology at the University of Memphis, who has authored over 30 books on grief and is a grief therapy trainer who developed the Meaning Making Model of Grief that focuses on integrating grief into the new version of our lives after loss.

In an interview with HealGrief, Neimeyer explains when we lose someone we are bonded to, we experience a tearing apart of our world of meaning that was anchored in that relationship.[6]

As we live our lives filled with memories of the past and hope for a shared future, Neimeyer explains, our lives with our parents get woven together. When our loved one is torn away from us through death, our life story is also torn apart.

What matters to us after that bond has been severed often comes under review.

Neimeyer says we naturally ask ourselves, sometimes for the first time, "Who am I now?" When our life is reduced, our sense of self is reduced. We wonder who our security base will be going forward and where we will find our refuge through storms.

If we were caregivers for our aging parents, we often find ourselves somewhat lost once the caregiving part of our life is over. The void that is left is vast.

"We are forced to change and rewrite our life stories that are changed and challenged by loss. That calls into question our basic life philosophy, spiritual views, existential questions," says Neimeyer. These aren't easily resolved and often require deep and personal reflection.

Trying to understand the world after loss is fundamental to our recovery.

Neimeyer says we are storytelling beings and "when the story of our life goes so profoundly wrong and critical players in that story are torn out of our lives, we have to rewrite every future chapter going forward because we don't have their physical presence with us."

Their physical absence requires a revision of our narrative, one that integrates our loved one's loss into our life story. To make meaning from this, we need to learn to live a life that honors them and keeps them alive.

"The good news of grief is, post-loss growth is a reality," says Neimeyer, "and it's displayed by a great many across time who deepen their compassion for the suffering of others, who come to be more tolerant of themselves, wiser about what matters in the long term, more self-aware regarding the significance of their own emotions and needs and that of others, and sometimes more alive in their spiritual lives or deeper in their philosophies."

There can be positive results that come from grief, besides the obvious tragic ones, if we make room for them.

Life *can* take on a deeper meaning.

"As human beings, we are wired for attachment in a world of impermanence," says Neimeyer. And so, we must rework the bond in a way that comforts us. We can take inspiration from our parents' lives, cultivate their best qualities inside ourselves, and revise, rather than relinquish, our bonds of love.

We can take steps toward healing when we find ways, big or small, to live a life that honors the imprints our parents left on us. Their life had meaning and always will.

Meaning is all about embracing life... after death.

If Not Now, When?

A favorite book of mine from years back was *The Artist's Way: A Spiritual Path to Higher Creativity*[7] by Julia Cameron, about prioritizing your creative life in a way that feels sustainable.

It came into my life as I was going through a big career pivot in my early thirties. I decided that following my heart was more important than a steady career, hard-earned accolades, a big paycheck, and a corner office on the 21st floor.

I put happiness over expectations and external validation.

The bottom line wasn't all that fulfilling to me anymore.

One of my favorite phrases in the book came from naturalist and essayist John Burroughs: *"Leap and the net will appear."*

At a time of transition, it encouraged me to take a risk, leave my comfort zone, and not be afraid of falling. Those three things, at that point, were completely against my nature.

But a time for new beginnings called and I answered.

The death of our parents brings on a similar call to action. It's a moment to rethink our choices in life, especially when we see how quickly time is moving forward.

It's about living from a soul level of awareness and shifting from a life on autopilot. Instead, start creating the life you want to live.

While the fear of dying was looming and big, I didn't want to fear living.

This point in the hero's journey is the part where we answer the call. *Our own call.*

As Alexa said, we can learn a lot by watching others who've been in our shoes. A short time after my last parent died, I had a wonderful conversation with my cousin, Karen. Even though I hadn't seen her in probably 40 years or more, it has been great getting to know the incredible person she is today, especially at this stage in both our lives.

Her parents both passed a few years prior, and she had been dealing with many of the same issues I had.

She also realized that when both of her parents passed, all that time spent doing it their way, the daily pressure she often felt about being a daughter and having to check in was now lifted. She first grieved deeply and eventually realized she could now do what *she* wanted to.

But what?

When we are used to putting our own needs second, like I did, that takes time to figure it out. Karen had to ask herself, "What do I like to do?" and actually wrote down a list of all the activities and kinds of places that brought her joy.

What she did next was to create a spectacular European vacation—free of obligation or anyone else's input—that included *all* the activities from her list.

She enjoyed beautiful gardens, morning markets, coastal walks, and ferry rides to nearby islands, several tidal isles, and stunning historical sites. She relaxed with lovely French breakfasts and savored the delicious local food. And was surrounded by nothing but kind people.

She took the leap to live her life with joy and she nailed it.

"I think that was a wonderful exercise to do it on my own, to take action for myself," she said. "And now, I *know* what I love to do. And if I give that to myself, I *do* create joy now. That is a step to the bigger question of 'Who am I now?'"

I was completely inspired and, with a smile, told her, "You're doing God's work just by living your life!" What a great example to follow.

Now I knew how to do it.

If I feel myself getting tentative about moving forward, I think about one of my favorite quotes from poet Erin Hanson: "There is a freedom waiting for you, on the breezes of the sky. And you ask, 'What if I fall?' Oh, but my darling, what if you fly?"[8]

Now is the time to establish your own art of living. Dare to find your joy.

Now is your time to fly.

INTENTION

I remember the moment, roughly two years after my mom died, when I woke up one morning, having hurt deeply, fully for so, so long, and feeling something other than a grieving heart. It was a new impulse. I had had enough.

I didn't want to be in pain anymore.

Back on that spring morning, it felt as if my mom was whispering to me just like she did when I was a little child, saying, "Come on, Honey, it's time to get up."

I heard it again—that same, literal "Wake up moment" one morning half a year after my dad died. The eight years of his decline, years spent exhausting myself caring for him before the torch was passed to my sister, four-hour roundtrips to see him after he moved in with her, and then grieving over him had all taken their toll.

I felt depleted by it all and thought, "I'm ready to feel better. I want a life; I want to live again."

I thought back to something that Michael Beckwith, a New Thought Minister, author, and founder of the Agape International Center in Beverly Hills, said that helped get me back on my feet after my mom's loss:

"Suffering is the great awakener. It is pain that becomes the impetus for genuine transformation."

What worked then was working again now. I sat with Beckwith's words and really took them in. In my gut, I was feeling a tingling of hopeful anticipation, not daily dread.

"Oh, yeah," I thought. "I'm ready. Let's do this."

With newfound intention, I had the motivating desire to heal and move forward.

POSITIVE MOTION

From everything I have lived, from everything I have learned from the toolbox tips that work for me, I know that starting my day needs to begin with peace, gratitude, and the clear intention to have a good day.

Calibrating my morning helps maintain positive momentum and balance.

In *Ask and It Is Given*,[9] by best-selling authors and new age teachers Esther Hicks and Jerry Hicks, based on the Universal Law of Attraction and the teachings of Abraham, when you align with Spirit (or God, Source energy, infinite intelligence, or whatever higher power means to you), you reawaken to the clarity, goodness, and power that is eternally you.

When I feel the natural flow, I feel good. When I don't, I feel bad. It's that simple.

"By consciously choosing the direction of your thoughts, you can be in constant connection with the Source energy, with God, with joy, and with all you consider to be good," according to Abraham.

I do what the teachings suggests; before even getting out of bed in the morning, I focus on the positive aspects of my life that I am grateful for. It begins with the most fundamental things: thankfulness for the soft pillow beneath my head, the cozy blankets that keep me warm, the roof above me, appreciation for the sun coming up, the beautiful colors of the flowers in my garden, the love of my animals, etc.

If I want to feel better, I keep reaching for better feelings and all that I have to be grateful for.

"Gratitude is a powerful catalyst for change,"[10] says Dr. Joe Dispenza, best-selling author and researcher who combines decades of studies into neuroscience, human biology, epigenetics, and quantum mechanics to present a process for rewiring the brain, creating new experiences, and healing.

Dispenza says that the doorway between our conscious and subconscious mind is wide open when we wake up in the morning and go to sleep at night. If you want to make changes in your life, these windows are opportunities to program and nurture our minds and bodies in new ways.

Many of the same principles taught by Hicks are seen in Dispenza's science-based—non "woo-woo"—work. Dispenza simply says, "What we practice, we get good at."

"You can learn and change in a state of pain and suffering," according to Dispenza, "or you can learn and change in a state of joy and inspiration." He advises us to make ourselves a priority, be a caregiver to ourselves, and make change as our own ally.

As I grew steadier on my emotional feet, I wanted to shape my experience with more intent. Instead of running on default from day to day, I consciously programmed new behaviors that would elevate my life.

In the course of his research, Dispenza found that instead of a positive start to the day, over 86 percent of people in the Western world begin their day with the stress-inducing habit of checking their cell phones for emails, texts, what's new on social media, and news updates.

By falling into this habitual morning routine, people allow the environment to condition their minds, feelings, and thoughts, and, in turn, in their body.

That often leads to chronic stress that negatively impacts their health and well-being.

Instead, he proposes a more intentional practice: Before you even get out of bed, think about how you'd like to feel and be that day. Rehearse it vividly in your mind. How and who would you like to be three or six months from now?

Strong, happy, fulfilled, optimistic, patient, energized—you name it.

See it, then *feel* what that would feel like. Picture what you would look like and the way you would act.

When I tried this, I could instantly feel the difference as my body flooded with happy hormones—just by imagining how a healed me would feel. According to Dispenza, in the same way athletes use visualization to train for success, rehearse for the person you want to be to prime the brain and body.

Once you know how to do this with your eyes closed, you can learn to do it with your eyes wide open, says Dispenza, as a walking meditation throughout your day.

According to researchers, the mind doesn't differentiate between memories, the present, or future visualizations. If it's vivid, the thoughts produce the same emotions and chemical reactions.

If you are thinking about the past, says Dispenza, your life will stay the same.

"Intentional morning routines can change your day and the direction of your life in a more positive way," he says.

As you move through your day, try to stay in a state of conscious awareness. If default patterns in the mind take over, stop, and make the shift. Create a new thought pattern, change your energy, and watch your elevated emotional state change your state of being.

This takes practice, but investing in ourselves is always worth it.

Signs you're doing it right include seeing your inside work impacting change in your outside world: you're sleeping better, there are "signs" and synchronicities (I can attest to this), things seem to be working out better for you, you are experiencing more elevated emotions, and you just *feel* better.

"Keep that up and you'll see instrumental changes in your life," says Dispenza. Then, "things start happening in your life to prove to you that you're actually the creator of your life instead of the victim of your life."

You hold the power to your well-being: "The best way to predict your future is to create it," as Dispenza says.

FIND YOUR SUNSHINE

Rumi follows the "sunshine principle."

When we gain momentum on our path forward, how do we know which road to take?

I'll share a couple of things a very wise Zen teacher taught me. That master, by the way, was my 22-year-old cat, Sashi (RIP, sweet girl).

Nothing could faze her. Not my nutso puppy who would get in her face to bark and play as she rested. The feline could let the wild energy pass her by like a mental jujitsu expert. She taught me, "Don't get pulled into someone else's crazy."

I would often find the master sitting in the garden, facing the sun, beside the blooming rose garden. I felt her say, as she sat in such a state of presence and tranquility, "When you watch a flower bloom, you are witnessing its ascension."

That cat was something.

But my favorite life lesson was one she demonstrated daily. Despite it being a cloudy day, she had a way of always finding that sliver of sunshine, either in a remote part of the house through a window or some obscure place in the yard.

She could always find the sunlight, curl up, and bask in its warmth.

She taught me, "We can't control the darkness, but we can search and find the light." Watching her so relaxed always felt like its own form of meditation.

"Find your sunshine," is what she taught by living.

You can too. As you move forward, remember to follow the sunshine principle, much like a sunflower follows the sunlight as it grows.

The Wounded Butterfly

As I progressed on my healing journey, I woke up feeling a little bit better each day.

I was using mindful practices, changing up my routine, and applying much of what I had learned since my dad's death.

The glass jar that held my grief had become larger as I had grown.

There were still mornings when I woke up with that uneasy sensation in the pit of my stomach, but I tuned into those feelings better now, telling them it'll be okay and imagining the day when there would be more joy and happiness again.

Before getting out of bed that day, I asked for a sign. "Please show me I'm on the right path."

Later that summer afternoon, I walked into my backyard and noticed a beautiful monarch butterfly in the shade on the stone pathway, unable to fly.

It broke my heart to watch it apparently dying. I then noticed water on the ground, and that its wings were wet and slightly damaged.

I had just read about how a butterfly won't fly in the rain or in a storm because water damages its wings and makes them too heavy to fly.

Butterflies also need a body temperature of 55°F, which means they must bask in direct sunlight to warm their flight muscles, regulate their body temperature, and dry their wings before flight.

I identified with that. I needed rest and self-regulation through my own emotional storm.

I moved the butterfly into the sun and sat next to it to make sure my curious onlooking cat didn't pounce on it. As I sat beside the wounded butterfly I told her, "It's okay. You're going to fly again, little one."

She started opening and closing her wings slowly—again and again—almost like she was taking deep breaths, growing a little stronger each time.

She wasn't dying; she just needed a pause where she was protected from a vulnerable situation, given a little love and encouragement, and time to grow stronger.

As she stumbled on her six legs, I named her Hope and softly told her, "You need to fly again, girl, for both of us."

Within 10 minutes in the warmth of the sun, she made an attempt to fly but faltered. I worried that I was engaged in magical thinking, and she wasn't really going to make it. She then slowly opened and closed her wings a few more times.

Finally, she did it. She flapped her wings several times and caught air. She flew low and fragile at first, but then she gained momentum and flew away.

Hope was soaring again!

I have a newfound respect for magical thinking, of new beginnings, and winks from the other side. I got the sign I asked for just earlier that morning. I looked up to the sky with a smile, the symbolism not lost on me, and said, "Thank you… thank you, thank you, thank you."

I got it.

I thought again about that famous C.S. Lewis quote. Throughout my grief journey, I did have to "sit with my anger long enough until she told me her real name was grief." I had to sit with other emotions as well for a time.

Now, I had sat with my cautious optimism long enough until she told me her name was Hope.

Does Time Heal All Wounds?

This is one of the most common questions, and the straight answer is there is no endpoint to grief. This is an emotional wound you feel on a soul level, and it will be there, in some form, as long as your love is alive.

Time alone is not a healer of pain; healing involves processing your grief in healthy ways. Denial, avoidance, and distraction won't help you ride your grief out. They'll just delay your healing.

I would say that what time does do is put space between the life-altering pain of your parents' loss and the room to adjust to life without them in their physical form.

It softens and gets easier in time, that I promise you.

But having loved and been loved will leave a mark. And it should.

The scar that remains is a tender badge of love.

CHAPTER 3

Rebirth

"Grief can be the garden of compassion. If you keep your heart open through everything, your pain can become your greatest ally in your life's search for love and wisdom."

— Rumi

LOSING BOTH PARENTS IS, WITHOUT question, a monumental life stage. It needs to be recognized and honored for that basic truth. Losing a big part of who we are can never be minimized, even with the passage of time.

The death of our parents marks a rebirth, a new life, and an awakening of a new you with new purpose and attributes.

The beginning of loss ushers in a turbulent deconstruction period; it brings emotional turmoil, a shakeup of our identity and our family of origin, priorities shift, mortality is faced, and life goals are re-examined.

People either grow together during this time or they grow apart.

We are all evolving works in progress through our lives, but never more so than after we lose both parents. And while the nature and intensity of grief will change—coming and going throughout our lifetime—we get better at moving with it.

Over the course of the grief journey, new strengths can emerge. Introspection can open us to a deeper world, and a balanced life becomes possible again.

Regardless of the time that elapses after your last parent dies, we seldom quite shake that initial feeling of being an orphan.

We adjust, and we do move forward, finding ways to incorporate our parents' memories into a new life we build for ourselves.

The New You

It's important to acknowledge that even when much is lost, so much can be learned through this healing process. We often find that we are all so much more capable and more resilient than we could have imagined.

Through this journey, we discover the value of the inner resources we have cultivated along the way:

We can be fearless, even in the face of insecurity.

We can be strong, even when we are vulnerable.

We can be decisive, even in the face of uncertainty.

We can show empathy, because we have endured pain.

And we can step into happiness again, because we have come to understand *it is our birthright.*

Grief can break us, or it can break us open. When we choose to take the core piece of who we were in that previous life and reconstruct a new version of ourselves—piece by piece, memory by memory—the beauty will be revealed.

We are all a magnificently unique mosaic of all the pieces that life experience has given us.

We are the result of all the love and heartbreaks, trials and triumphs, friendships and betrayals, pain and joy, tears and laughter, and everything that this human experience has laid before us.

There was never anything to prove or earn. The end of the journey is coming back home to the authentic you.

Fly

This book has journeyed through the altered life we confront after our parents' death, through the complicated grieving process, to our rebirth into a new world and life that follows.

It is a transformative, introspective passage that begins with that lonely "orphaned" feeling associated with double parental loss. These pages have, hopefully, taken you through steps that will assist in processing your love and loss, and finding your way forward.

When you are ready, it will be a unique chance to create the next stage in life for yourself. What dreams will you follow? What legacy do you want to leave?

This marks a time of endless possibilities, and yet natural fears of the unknown will still arise at times. That's okay. That's normal. The path forward won't be a tidy sequence of steps without bumps along the way.

Healing takes an act of grace.

When you give yourself that gift, you can do anything.

At this point in your personal story, you probably have a deeper appreciation for the fragility of life, what really matters, and that the time left is finite. You are the one who will write the next chapters.

As you step into this new beginning, toss all "shoulds" aside and stay open. Chart your own path. Explore. Take chances. Love boldly. Be curious. Be kind. Stay patient and rest when you need to. Leave memories, not regrets.

Breathe life in deeply... and live!

Your life narrative has an arc, and it has brought you here.

You decide your next steps. Let this book serve as your faithful sherpa anytime you need guidance, support, encouragement, or gentle reminders again.

And like the stack of rocks called *cairns* (the Scottish Gaelic word meaning "heap of stones") that serve as markers in nature along walking paths or beach trails, let it also serve as a compass on your journey forward.

It will be here for you whenever you need a companion and guide. For now, rest. When you are ready, you will get up again. There is power in the pause. Take it.

And when the moment comes and your wings are dry again, take a leap and dare to soar...

You are the butterfly.

ACKNOWLEDGMENT

Excerpt for "The Prayer" Lyrics

I pray you'll be our eyes, and watch us where we go
And help us to be wise in times when we don't know
Let this be our prayer, when we lose our way
Lead us to the place, guide us with your grace
To a place where we'll be safe

I pray we'll find your light, and hold it in our hearts
When stars go out each night,
Remind us where you are
Let this be our prayer, when shadows fill our day
Help us find a place, guide us with your grace
Give us faith so we'll be safe

Written by: David Foster, Carole Bayer Sager, Alberto Testa, and Tony Renis
Copyright: Lyrics © Warner/Chappell Music, Inc.

My hope is that everyone holding this book and reading these pages feels the never-ending presence from their parents above, and that they continue to light your way.

May you always feel and continue to grow that connection, or, in some cases, take with you the lessons that made you who you are despite circumstances.

I want to extend a very special thank you to those who have shared their own experience of loss, vulnerability, fears, and stories of strength and perseverance. I am inspired by such kind, heart-centered people—some of whom are friends, some family, some professionals, and many times total strangers.

Special thanks to Jim Endrst and Brent Atwater for your personal and professional guidance; Laura Wilson for your steadfast friendship and emotional support; Karen Rakestraw, Shyrl Lorino, Kim Wilder, Linda Keefer, Judy Torres, Michael DiPasquale, Theresa Crawford, Janet Jordon, Susan Dost, Annette Hoffman, and Mary Costa for showing up in such invaluable ways; and P. J. Canady, Diane Leah, and Cyn Edwards for your friendship and unwavering commitment to our support group despite your own heartbreaks.

I am forever grateful for the breadth of compassion and humanity I've been shown by so many.

As I've said before, *love will break your heart, but it will also heal it.*

That truth endures.

ABOUT THE AUTHOR

Elaine Mallon

AUTHOR **ELAINE MALLON** KNOWS THE magnitude and overwhelming heartbreak of losing parents firsthand. With deep empathy for those who might feel lost, misunderstood, or alone after the death of their mother, Elaine felt compelled to write the compassionate grief recovery guidebook she desperately needed when her own mom unexpectedly died. After her father's passing eight years later, she followed up with a second book about navigating double parental loss and entering this new stage in life as an "adult orphan," a topic seldom explored in literature on grief.

Her first book, *Healing After the Loss of Your Mother: A Grief & Comfort Manual*—recognized as one of the Best Grief Books of All Time by BookAuthority—is a heartfelt and practical guidebook for those mourning the loss of their mother and for supporters hoping to help a loved one through grief.

Since its launch in 2018, the acclaimed self-help book has consistently been an Amazon Best Seller in several categories, including Grief & Bereavement, Mental & Spiritual Healing, Love & Loss, and Sociology of Death.

Healing After the Loss of Your Parents: Finding Comfort & Purpose Through This New Life Stage as an Adult Orphan is a natural follow-up to her first book. This comprehensive and insightful grief recovery guidebook helps readers navigate through the disorienting "natural rite of passage" and cope with the profound changes that follow the death of their parents, empowering them to rebuild their life after loss.

Both books provide a road map through heartache... toward hope and healing.

In addition to writing, Mallon is a grief support advocate who founded two bereavement groups as companions to each book. In 2016, she established Healing After the Loss of Your Mother – Grief Support (approximately 25,000 members worldwide), and in 2024, formed Healing After the Loss of Your Parents – Grief Support. Both online groups are sacred spaces for those seeking comfort and community through their loss. They are free and available 24 hours a day, 7 days a week, 365 days a year on Facebook.

Elaine Mallon is an award-winning public relations and marketing veteran who began her professional career in entertainment publicity and later became Vice President, Media & Corporate Relations at 20th Century Fox Television.

She resides in Los Angeles, California.

My mother, Irma   My father, Dennis

LINKS & HELPFUL RESOURCES

The Suicide Prevention Lifeline: SuicidePreventionLifeline.org
International Association for Suicide Prevention: iasp.info
National Institute of Mental Health: nlm.nih.gov
Hospice Foundation of America: HospiceFoundation.org
American Hospice Foundation: AmericanHospice.org
Center for Loss & Life Transitions: centerforloss.com
What's Your Grief: WhatsYourGrief.com
Grief.com: Grief.com
GriefShare: GriefShare.org
HealGrief: HealGrief.org
HelpGuide: HelpGuide.org
The Grief Channel: https://www.youtube.com/@griefchannel
Harvard Health Medical Newsletter: Health.Harvard.edu
Psychology Today: PsychologyToday.com
Eckhart Tolle: eckharttolle.com
Brené Brown: brenebrown.com
Well+Good: wellandgood.com
Cindy Bentley: dnareconnection.com
Karen Hager: karenhager.com
Brent Atwater: brentatwater.com
American Bar Association: americanbar.org
National Hospice and Palliative Care Organization: caringinfo@nhpco.org
Prepare for Your Care: prepareforyourcare.org
Vietnam Veterans of America (Tax Deductible Donations/Free Pickup): scheduleapickup.com
NBC News original "How Grief Affects Your Brain and What to Do About It": https://www.youtube.com/watch?v=eEcaUhx

AH2g&list=PL25HNlgTOQqbeAhnPVQEp1rAtpjpGkRtw&index=15

Megan Devine "How to Help a Grieving Friend: The Animation (Video): https://www.youtube.com/watch?v=l2zLCCRT-nE

Healing After the Loss of Your Mother – Grief Support: www.facebook.com/groups/299570487047231

Healing After the Loss of Your Parents – Grief Support Group: www.facebook.com/groups/740088704595326

NOTES

INTRODUCTION

1. Dorian Mauro, "I Miss You" in French: Definition, Synonyms, and Examples," French Iceberg, 2023, https://french-iceberg.com/i-miss-you-in-french
2. Elaine Mallon, *Healing After the Loss of Your Mother: A Grief & Comfort Manual* (E. Mallon, 2018).
3. George Hayward, "New 2021 Data Visualization Shows Parent Mortality 44.2% Had Lost at Least One Parent., United States Census Bureau, 2023, https://french-iceberg.com/i-miss-you-in-french.

PART I: THE ADULT ORPHAN

CHAPTER 1: LOSING BOTH PARENTS

1. "Well Known Expressions," BookBrowse, https://www.bookbrowse.com/expressions/detail/index.cfm/expression_number/120/home-is-where-the-heart-is
2. Debra Umberson, *Death of a Parent: Transition to a New Adult Identity* (Cambridge University Press, 2003).
3. Shoba Sreenivasan, PhD, and Linda E. Weinberger, PhD, "When Both Elderly Parents Die: The Complex Psychological Journey of Becoming an Orphan Late in Life," *Psychology Today*, 2023,

4. https://www.psychologytoday.com/us/blog/emotional-nourishment/202307/when-both-elderly-parents-die.
5. Michelle Hamer, "The Peculiar Grief of the Adult Orphan," *The Age*,
6. https://www.theage.com.au/national/the-peculiar-grief-of-the-adult-orphan-20030908-gdwaws.html.
7. Alexander Levy, *The Orphaned Adult* (Hachette Books, 1999).
8. Julia Samuel, *Grief Works: Stories of Life, Death and Surviving* (Scribner, 2017).
9. Jane Brooks, *Midlife Orphan: Facing Life's Challenges Now That Your Parents are Gone* (Berkley Books, 1999).
10. Alexander Levy, *The Orphaned Adult* (Hachette Books, 1999).
11. Jane Brooks, *Midlife Orphan: Facing Life's Challenges Now That Your Parents are Gone* (Berkley Books, 1999).
12. Lisa M. Shulman, *Before and After Loss: A Neurologist's Perspective on Loss, Grief, and Our Brain* (John Hopkins University Press, 2018).
13. Debra Umberson, *Death of a Parent: Transition to a New Adult Identity* (Cambridge University Press, 2003).
14. The National Institute on Aging, "Getting Your Affairs in Order Checklist: Documents to Prepare for the Future," February 1, 2023.. https://www.nia.nih.gov/health/advance-care-planning/getting-your-affairs-order-checklist-documents-prepare-future.

Chapter 2: The Grieving Process

1. Dr. Alan Wolfelt, Center for Loss & Life Transitions, https://www.CenterForLoss.com.

2. Patrick Tyrell, Seneca Harberger, Caroline Schoo, and Waquar Siddiqui, "Kübler-Ross Stages of Dying and Subsequent Models of Grief," National Library of Medicine, https://www.ncbi.nlm.nih.gov/books/NBK507885/.
3. Elisabeth Kübler-Ross, MD, *On Death & Dying* (Scribner, reissue 2014).
4. Angela Morrow, RN, "5 Stages of Grief When Facing a Terminal Diagnosis Understanding the Kübler-Ross Model," Verywell Health. https://www.verywellhealth.com/dabda-the-five-stages-of-coping-with-death-1132148
5. Elisabeth Kübler-Ross and David Kessler, *On Grief & Grieving: Finding the Meaning of Grief Through the Five Stages of Loss* (Simon & Schuster, 2005).
6. William J. Worden,, *Grief Counseling and Grief Therapy: A Handbook for the Mental Health Practitioner, Fifth Edition* (Springer, 2018).
7. Lois Tonkin, TTC, "Growing around Grief—Another Way of Looking at Grief and Recovery," *Bereavement Care* 15 (1): 10 https://www.tandfonline.com/doi/abs/10.1080/02682629608657376.
8. The Ralph Site, Diagram: Growing around grief, http://theralphsiteshop.com/moving-forward-not-moving-on/.
9. Dr. Jenni Jacobsen, PhD, LSW, "5 Best-Known Grief Theories and Models," Calmerry, https://calmerry.com/blog/grief-and-loss/top-grief-theories-and-models/

CHAPTER 3: EMPOWERED GRIEVING

1. Ian J. Hamilton, "Theories of Grief," National Library of Medicine, 2024, https://www.ncbi.nlm.nih.gov/pmc/articles/

PMC5033290/#:~:text=Freud1%20proposed%20the%20original,circumstances%2C%20and%20building%20new%20relationships.
2. Dr. Michael Baker, "What Is Grief Work?" GEC, 2022, https://mygec.org/2022/03/16/what-is-grief-work.
3. Eckhart Tolle, *The Power of Now* (New World Library and Namaste Publishing, 1977).

Chapter 4: Where to Start?

1. Julie Samuel, *Grief Works: Stories of Life, Death, and Surviving* (Scribner, 2017).
2. Elaine Mallon, *Healing After the Loss of Your Mother: A Grief & Comfort Manual* (Elaine Mallon, 2018).

Chapter 6: How Grief Rewires the Brain

1. NBC News, "How Grief Affects Your Brain and What to Do About It," June 14, 2018, https://www.youtube.com/watch?v=eEcaUhxAH2g&list=PL25HNlgTOQqbeAhnPVQEp1rAtpjpGkRtw&index=15.
2. Lisa M. Shulman, *Before and After Loss: A Neurologist's Perspective on Loss, Grief And Our Brain*, (John Hopkins University Press, 2018).
3. Lisa M. Shulman, *Before and After Loss: A Neurologist's Perspective on Loss, Grief And Our Brain* (John Hopkins University Press, 2018).
4. Yosh Solanki, "Neuroplasticity: Examples—What is Neuroplasticity," Study.com, 2024, https://study.com/buy/academy/lesson/

what-is-neuroplasticity-definition-depression-quiz.html?src=ppc_bing_nonbrand&rcntxt=aws&crt=&kwd=SEO-PPC-BUY&kwid=dat-2329040505886940:loc190&agid=1235851302596746&mt=b&device=c&network=o&_campaign=SeoPPC&msclkid=63d757d062bc1e42dd3a31af7f462583.

5. Claire Bidwell Smith, LCPC, *Conscious Grieving: A Transformative Approach to Healing from Loss* (Workman Publishing Co., 2024).
6. Josep Calbet, "Hebb's Rule with an Analogy: Psychology and Neuroscience," *The Quotient Blog*, 2018, https://neuroquotient.com/en/pshychology-and-neuroscience-hebb-principle-rule/.
7. Tara Swart, *The Source: The Secrets of the Universe, the Science of the Brain* (Harper One, 2019).
8. NBC News, "How Grief Affects Your Brain and What to Do About It," June 14, 2018, https://www.youtube.com/watch?v=eEcaUhxAH2g&list=PL25HNlgTOQqbeAhnPVQEplrAtpjpGkRtw&index=15.
9. Courtney E. Ackerman, MA, "What Is Neuroplasticity: A Psychologist Explains," *PositivePsychology*, https://positivepsychology.com/neuroplasticity/.
10. Traci Pedersen, "What Does Grief Do to Your Brain?" PsychCentral, 2022, https://psychcentral.com/lib/your-health-and-grief.
11. Courtney E. Ackerman, MA, "What Is Neuroplasticity: A Psychologist Explains," *PositivePschology*, 2024, https://positivepsychology.com/neuroplasticity/.
12. Tchicki Davis, PhD, "The Hormones that Boost Happiness: Learn More About Dopamine, Serotonin, Oxytocin, and Endorphins," *Psychology Today*, 2024, https://www.psychologytoday.com/gb/blog/click-here-for-happiness/202312/hormones-that-boost-happiness.

Chapter 7: Grief Versus Depression

1. Cecilia Effa, "What is the Difference Between Depression and Grief," Medical News Today, 2023, https://www.medicalnewstoday.com/articles/depression-vs-grief#differences.
2. Daniel K. Hall-Flavin, MD, "Clinical Depression: What Does it Mean?" Mayo Clinic, 2017, https://www.mayoclinic.org/diseases-conditions/depression/expert-answers/clinical-depression/faq-20057770.
3. Mary-Francis O'Connor, *The Grieving Brain: The Surprising Science of How We Learn from Love and Loss,* (Harper One, 2023).
4. Hospice of the Red River Valley, "The Difference Between Grief and Depression," 2017, file:///C:/Users/elain/Downloads/Grief-vs.-Depression_What-to-Know-and-When-to-Seek-Help_1217.pdf.
5. Alexandra Benisek, "What is Prolonged Grief Disorder?" WebMd, 2024, https://www.webmd.com/mental-health/prolonged-grief-disorder.
6. Paul Appelbaum, MD, and Lamyaa Yousif, MD, PhD, "Prolonged Grief Disorder," American Psychiatric Association, https://www.psychiatry.org/patients-families/prolonged-grief-disorder.
7. Alexandra Cromer, LPC, "How Long Does Grief Last?" Thriveworks, https://thriveworks.com/grief-loss/how-long-does-grief-last.
8. Cynthia Vinney, PhD, "Anticipatory Grief is Actually a Thing – What to Know About It," Verywell Mind, 2023. https://www.verywellmind.com/what-is-anticipatory-grief/5207928.

9. Litsa Williams, "Grieving Before Death: Understanding Anticipatory Grief," What's Your Grief? 2013, https://www.whatsyourgrief.com/anticipatory-grief/.
10. Litsa Williams, "Grieving Before Death: Understanding Anticipatory Grief," What's Your Grief? 2013, https://whatsyourgrief.com/anticipatory-grief/.
11. Angela Morrow, RN, "Difference Between Normal and Complicated Grief," Verywell Health, 2023, https://www.verywellhealth.com/grief-and-mourning-process-1132545.
12. Rhitu Chatterjee, "The New 988 Mental Health Hotline is Live. Here's What to Know," NPR, 2022, https://www.npr.org/sections/health-shots/2022/07/15/1111316589/988-suicide-hotline-number.
13. Amy Marturana Winderl, CPT, "How to Tell the Difference Between Sadness, Grief, and Depression," *Self*, 2016, https://www.self.com/story/the-difference-between-sadness-grief-depression.
14. Elisabeth Kübler-Ross and David Kessler, *On Grief & Grieving: Finding the Meaning of Grief Through the Five Stages of Loss* (Simon & Schuster, 2005).

Chapter 8: How Long Will This Pain Last?

1. US Department of Labor, "Federal Law," 2024, www.dol.gov/general/topic/benefits-leave/funeral-leave.

Chapter 9: Grief Triggers & Glimmers

1. Lauren Presutti, "Dealing with Grief Triggers: Understanding and Managing Reminders of Loss," *River Oaks Psychology*, https://riveroakspsychology.com/dealing-with-grief-triggers-understanding-and-managing-reminders-of-loss/.
2. Natalie Gale, "How Glimmers Can Eliminate Our Triggers," The Good Trade, 2023, (https://www.thegoodtrade.com/features/glimmers-and-triggers/.
3. Newport Institute. "What Are Glimmers and Why Are They Good For You?" 2023, https://www.newportinstitute.com/resources/mental-health/what-are-glimmers/.
4. Newport Institute. "What Are Glimmers and Why Are They Good For You?" 2023, https://www.newportinstitute.com/resources/mental-health/what-are-glimmers/.

Chapter 12: The Afterlife

1. Adam Volle, Britannica, "Afterlife." 2024, https://www.britannica.com/topic/spirituality.
2. J. Cannon. "Life After Death: The Other Side," Dolores Cannon, http://dolorescannon.com/life-death-side/.
3. Dolores Cannon, "Dolores Cannon on Life After Death," YouTube, 2015, https://www.youtube.com/watch?v=FhjoEnG4gww.
4. Dolores Cannon, "Dolores Cannon on Life After Death," YouTube, 2015, https://www.youtube.com/watch?v=FhjoEnG4gww.

5. Jeffrey Long, MD, "Near Death Experience Evidence for Their Reality," National Library of Medicine, https://www.ncbi.nlm.nih.gov/pmc/articles/PMC6172100/.
6. Wikipedia, "Raymond Moody," https://en.wikipedia.org/wiki/Raymond_Moody.
7. The Intuition Network, "Thinking Allowed, Conversations on the Leading Edge of Knowledge and Discovery, with Dr. Jeffrey Mishlove," http://www.intuition.org/txt/moody.htm.
8. *The Afterlife*. Full Documentary. Directed by Paul Perry, YouTube, https://www.youtube.com/watch?v=8aWveRxcVP8.
9. Melanie Beckler. "How to tell the difference between visitation dreams and regular dreams," Ask Angels, https://www.ask-angels.com/spiritual-guidance/visitation-dreams/.
10. Brent Atwater, *Lessons from Loved Ones in Heaven: How to Connect with your Loved One on the Other Side to Heal from Loss* (Just Plain Love Books, 2000-2018).
11. Laura Lynn Jackson, *Signs: The Secret Language of the Universe*. (The Dial Press, 2019).
12. Tanya Carroll Richardson, "18 Examples of Synchronicities & What to Do When They Happen to You," Mindbodygreen, https://www.mindbodygreen.com/articles/synchronicities.

Chapter 13: Coping Tools, Tips & Strategies

1. Judith Orloff, "The Health Benefits of Tears" *Psychology Today*, 2010, https://www.psychologytoday.com/intl/blog/emotional-freedom/201007/the-health-benefits-tears
2. Erin Bunch, "Stop Screaming Inside Your Heart, and Use Scream Therapy to Let it Out," *Well+Good*, 2020, https://www.wellandgood.com/scream-therapy/.

3. Esther Hicks and Jerry Hicks, *The Law of Attraction* (Hay House 2006).
4. Megan Hoffner, MM MT-BC, Julie Avirett, MM MT-BC, Kelsey Bocharski, and Joshua Da Costa, "How Music Affects Your Mind, Mood and Body," Tallahassee Memorial Healthcare, 2022, https://www.tmh.org/heathly-living/blogs/healthy-living/how-music-affects-your-mnd-mood-and-body.
5. Gina Vivinetto, "Watching Our Favorite TV Shows Has Psychological Benefits," *The Today Show*, 2019, https://www.today.com/health/watching-nostalgia-tv-has-psychological-benefits-experts-say-t157090.
6. Pathways, "Bereavement and Grief Don't Exclude Laughter," 2024, https://www.pathwayshealth.org/bereavement-grief-doesn't-exclude-laughter.
7. Jennifer Haupt, "How Pets Helps Us Grieve," *Psychology Today*, 2021, https://www.psychologytoday.com/us/blog/one-true-thing/202110/how-pets-help-us-grieve.
8. Michelle Harler, "Why Do Cats Purr? The Mystery Behind the Comforting Sound," MSN, 2024, https://www.msn.com/en-us/health/other/why-do-cats-purr-the-mystery-behind-the-comforting-sound/ar-BB1lvE28.
9. CDC, "How Much Sleep," https://www.cdc.gov/sleep/about_sleep/how_much_sleep.html.
10. Mindful.org, "How to Meditate," https://www.mindful.org/how-to-meditate/.
11. Kristen Fischer, "Grounding: Techniques and Benefits," WebMD, https://balance/grounding-benefits.
12. The Cell Health Team, "The Science Behind Ocean Negative Ions and Their Health Benefits," *Cell Health News*, https://cellhealthnews.com/articles/the-science-behind-ocean-negative-ions/.

Part III: How to Support Someone Who Is Grieving

Chapter 1: Comfort 101

1. David Kessler, *Finding Meaning: The Sixth Stage of Grief* (Simon & Schuster, 2019).
2. Merriam-Webster Dictionary, "Empathy," 2024, https://www.merriam-webster.com/dictionary/empathy.
3. Brené Brown, *Daring Greatly: How the Courage to Be Vulnerable Transforms the Way We Live, Love, Parent, and Lead* (Random House, 2018).
4. Merriam-Webster Dictionary. "Compassion," 2024, https://www.merriam-webster.com/dictionary/compassion.
5. Merriam-Webster Dictionary, "Sympathy," 2024, https://www.merriam-webster.com/dictionary/sympathy.

Chapter 6: You Can't Pour from an Empty Cup

1. Kendry Cherry, MSEd, "Compassion vs. Empathy: What's the Difference?" Verywell Mind, 2023, https://www.verywellmind.com/compassion-vs-empathy-what-s-the-difference-7494906.

Part IV: Purpose & the Path Forward

Chapter 1: The Arc of Life

1. Pema Chödrön, *Embracing the Unknown: Life Lessons from the Tibetan Book of the Dead* (Sounds True, 2019).

2. Pema Chödrön, *When Things Fall Apart: Heart Advice for Difficult Times* (Shambhala, 2016).

Chapter 2: The Hero's Journey

1. Joseph Campbell, *The Hero with a Thousand Faces* (Princeton University Press, 1972).
2. Mel Robbins, "How to Make Your Life Exciting Again," YouTube, 2014, https://www.youtube.com/watch?v=awLRiNhrNis&t=301s.
3. Dave Roos, "Victor Frankl's Search for Meaning in 5 Enduring Quotes," HowStuffWorks, https://history.howstuffworks.com/historical-figures/viktor-frankl.htm.
4. Eckhart Tolle, *A New Earth: Awakening to Your Life's Purpose* (Penguin Group, 2006).
5. Lisa M. Shulman, *Before and After Loss: A Neurologist's Perspective on Loss, Grief, and Our Brain* (John Hopkins University Press, 2018).
6. Robert Neimeyer, "Let's Talk Death with Robert Neimeyer, PhD," HealGrief, YouTube, 2019, https://www.youtube.com/watch?v=3TqHNertUlQ.
7. Julia Cameron, *The Artist's Way: A Spiritual Path to Higher Creativity* (Tarcher, 1992).
8. Erin Hanson, Goodreads quote, 2024, https://www.goodreads.com/author/quotes/7802403.Erin_Hanson.
9. Esther Hicks and Jerry Hicks, *Ask and It Is Given: Learning to Manifest Your Desires* (Hay House, Inc. 2004).
10. Dr. Rangan Chatterjee, "Do This First Thing in the Morning to Brainwash Yourself for Success | Dr. Joe Dispenza," YouTube, 2023, https://www.youtube.com/watch?v=Z3Alav9Jig0.

BONUS SECTION

YOUR PERSONAL JOURNALING PAGES

*"What the caterpillar calls the end of the
world the master calls a butterfly."*

— RICHARD BACH

Journaling is a powerful aid in grief recovery and healing. These pages are your private, safe space for stream of consciousness writing. This is a no judgment zone.

The written word can help to process and better understand intense feelings and private thoughts. It's a powerful release method.

Tip: Use a favorite photo or photos of your parents as bookmarks to this section. Breathe deeply, feel their presence, and perhaps ask for their guidance in your healing process.

Your private journaling pages include areas for:

- Notes to Myself
- Favorite Glimmers & Signs
- Parental Life Lessons & Advice
- Gratitude Journal

"The most important journey you will take in your life will usually be the one of self-transformation."

— SHANNON L. ALDER

NOTES TO MYSELF:

Please use this space to express thoughts that emerge while reading this book or to write down useful tips and insights you found especially helpful.

_____

_____

_____

_____

_____

_____

_____

Healing After the Loss of Your Parents

Healing After the Loss of Your Parents

Elaine Mallon

Healing After the Loss of Your Parents

> *"I have always been delighted at the prospect of a new day, a fresh try, one more start, with perhaps a bit of magic waiting somewhere behind the morning."*
>
> — J. B. Priestley

Favorite Glimmers & Signs:

Have you felt your parents' presence through signs, dreams, synchronicity, or glimmers that simply fill you with joy?

Write these comforting and uplifting occurrences down. Remember them. Revisit these pages whenever you need to feel connected and hopeful.

_____

_____

_____

_____

_____

Healing After the Loss of Your Parents

Elaine Mallon

Healing After the Loss of Your Parents

Elaine Mallon

Healing After the Loss of Your Parents

"No matter how far we come, our parents are always in us."

— Brad Meltzer

Parental Life Lessons & Advice:

As you read and reflect on this book, old memories will likely come up.

Use this section to record some of your parents' most helpful words of wisdom, big or small. What life lessons did they teach you that you hope to carry forward? What memories always fill you with warmth?

Reflect on happy times when you are feeling low. Also, if you embody their best qualities, you will carry their insight forward and possibly help others. Let them continue to live through you.

_____

_____

_____

_____

_____

Healing After the Loss of Your Parents

Elaine Mallon

Healing After the Loss of Your Parents

Elaine Mallon

Healing After the Loss of Your Parents

"Appreciation can make a day, even change a life. Your willingness, put into words is all that is necessary."

— MARGARET COUSINS

GRATITUDE JOURNAL:

Being in a state of thankfulness for the good things in life can have a profound impact on your mental and physical well-being. When you experience gratitude, your mind, body, and soul respond with feelings of warmth, kindness, and peace.

According to wellness experts, when we express gratitude, our brain releases dopamine and serotonin, the two crucial neurotransmitters responsible for the emotions that make us feel *good*.

Remember to always be grateful for the things you have, no matter how big or small.

The more mindfully you observe, the more you'll notice.

Reflecting on these observations can sometimes help when you are struggling or feeling low. As you re-read these journal pages, it will be *you... comforting yourself.*

Healing After the Loss of Your Parents

Healing After the Loss of Your Parents

Elaine Mallon

Healing After the Loss of Your Parents

Elaine Mallon

www.ingramcontent.com/pod-product-compliance
Lightning Source LLC
Chambersburg PA
CBHW072146070526
44585CB00015B/1017